AF225716

ISBN 978-0-6481964-0-2

General enquiries
info@1000tales.org.au
(+61) 481 571 595

Shop
www.1000tales.org.au/shop

Contributors

Arulanantham Jeevatharshan

Atiya Karimshah

Donbosco Prashanth

Johana Bueno

Johnny Nguyễn

Krushanth Thanabalasingam

Mayra Alejandra Abadia Quimbaya

Nguyễn Ngọc Dũng

Shabnaaz Sheik Ahmed

Trine Vik

Editorial

Ameera Krushanth

Cover Design

Shabnaaz Sheik Ahmed

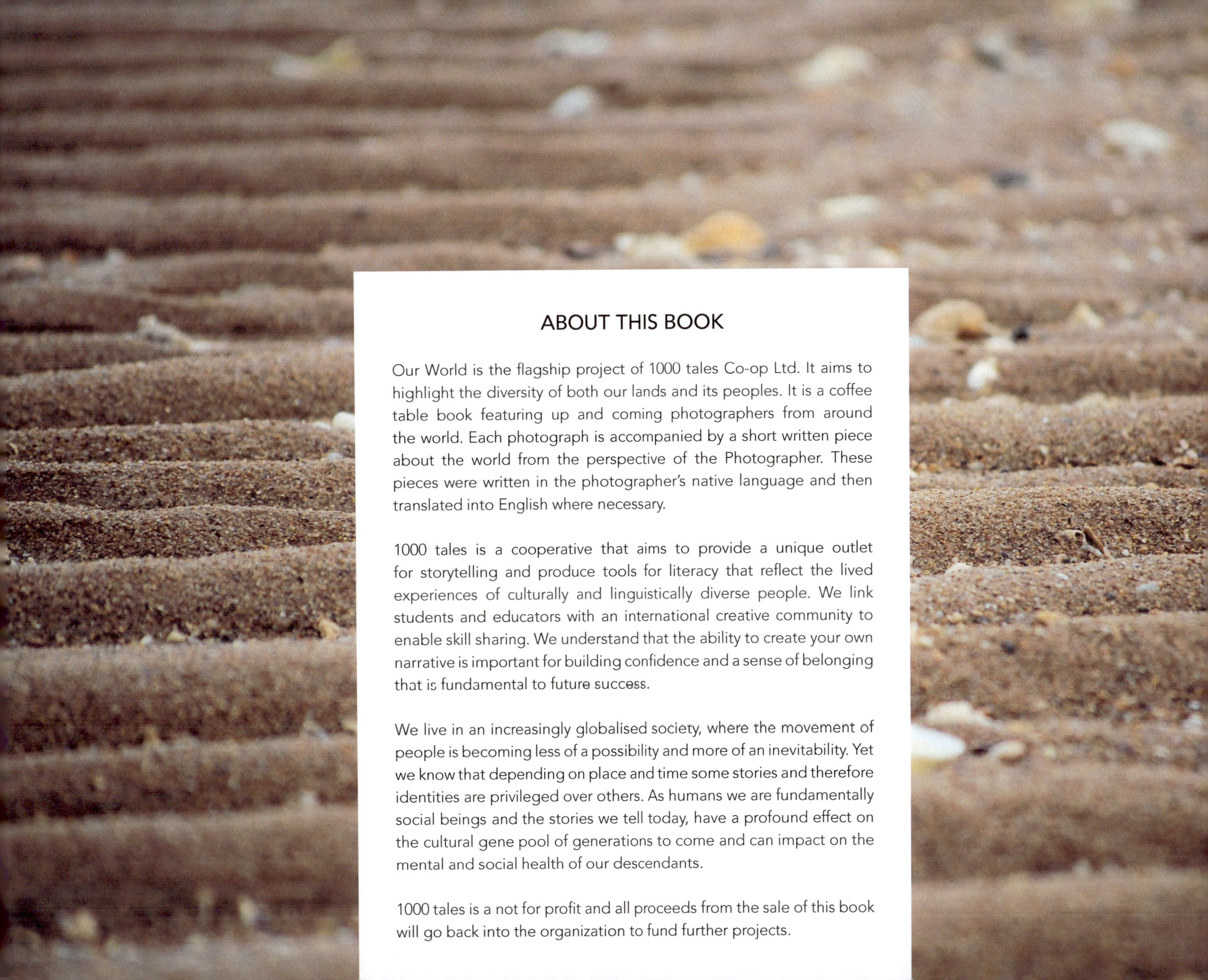

ABOUT THIS BOOK

Our World is the flagship project of 1000 tales Co-op Ltd. It aims to highlight the diversity of both our lands and its peoples. It is a coffee table book featuring up and coming photographers from around the world. Each photograph is accompanied by a short written piece about the world from the perspective of the Photographer. These pieces were written in the photographer's native language and then translated into English where necessary.

1000 tales is a cooperative that aims to provide a unique outlet for storytelling and produce tools for literacy that reflect the lived experiences of culturally and linguistically diverse people. We link students and educators with an international creative community to enable skill sharing. We understand that the ability to create your own narrative is important for building confidence and a sense of belonging that is fundamental to future success.

We live in an increasingly globalised society, where the movement of people is becoming less of a possibility and more of an inevitability. Yet we know that depending on place and time some stories and therefore identities are privileged over others. As humans we are fundamentally social beings and the stories we tell today, have a profound effect on the cultural gene pool of generations to come and can impact on the mental and social health of our descendants.

1000 tales is a not for profit and all proceeds from the sale of this book will go back into the organization to fund further projects.

Aurora

Ein lett dans
Som ingen andre kan
På det mørkraste lerretet
I eit kaldt og nordleg land
Ei framsyning for alle
Og ingen tar betalt
For kven eig naturen?
Og dei strøka som usynlege penslar
har malt.

Photography by: Trine Vik
Norway

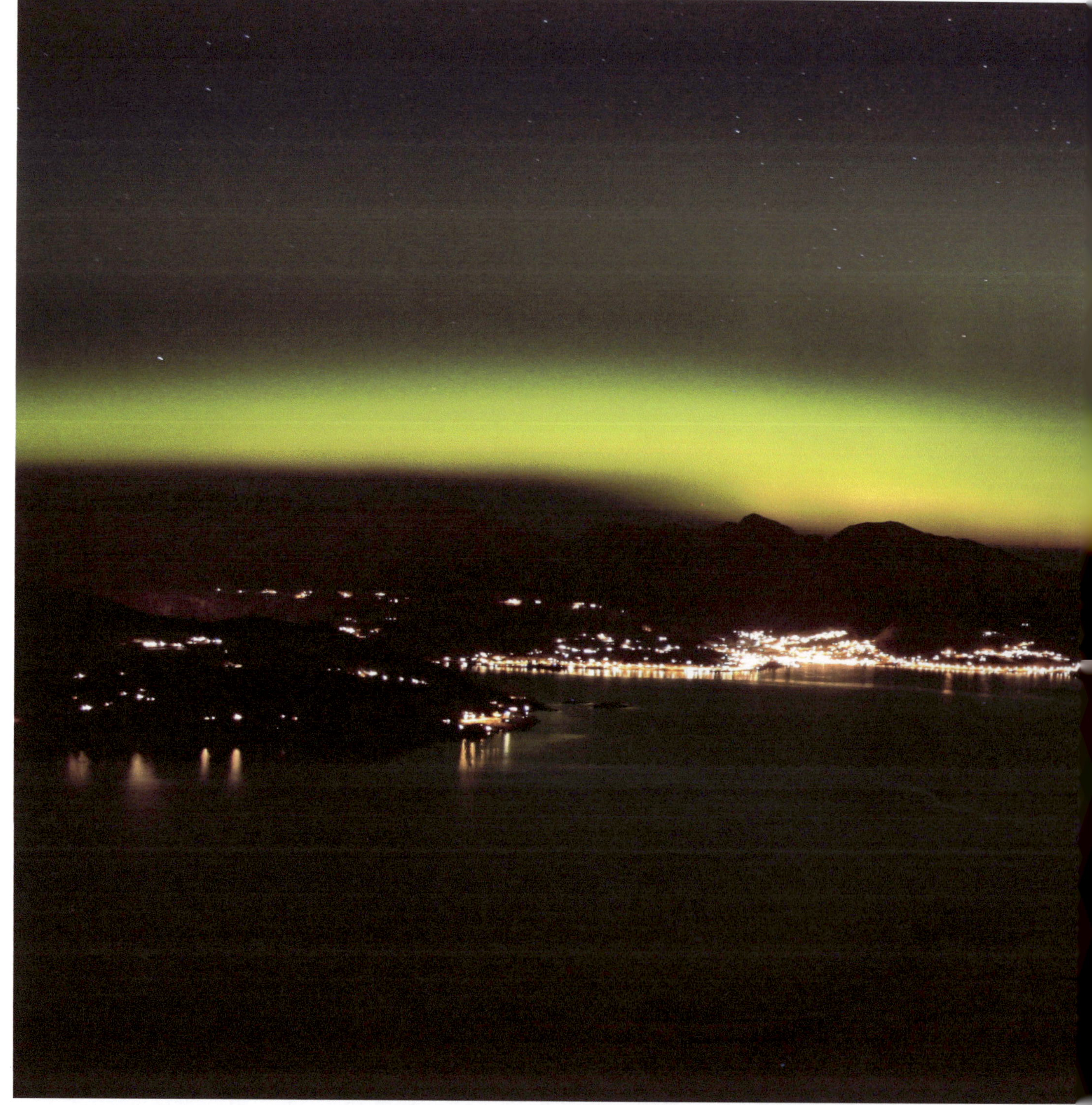

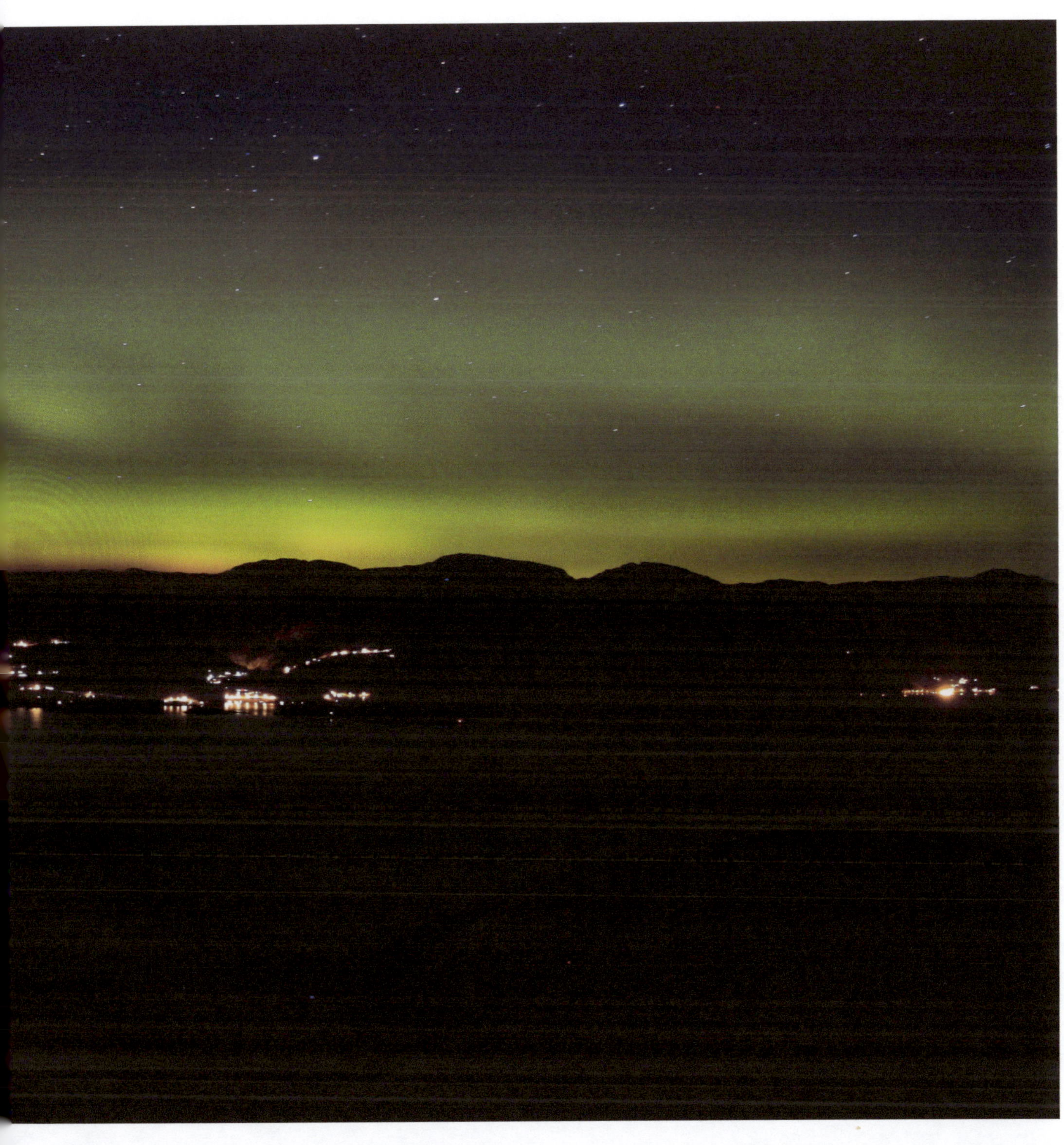

Aurora

A luminous dance
Of shimmering rays
On the darkest of canvases
In a cold and northern place
Invisible brushes paint
In shades of green and gold
A show for us all
But with no tickets sold

Poem & translation by Trine Vik

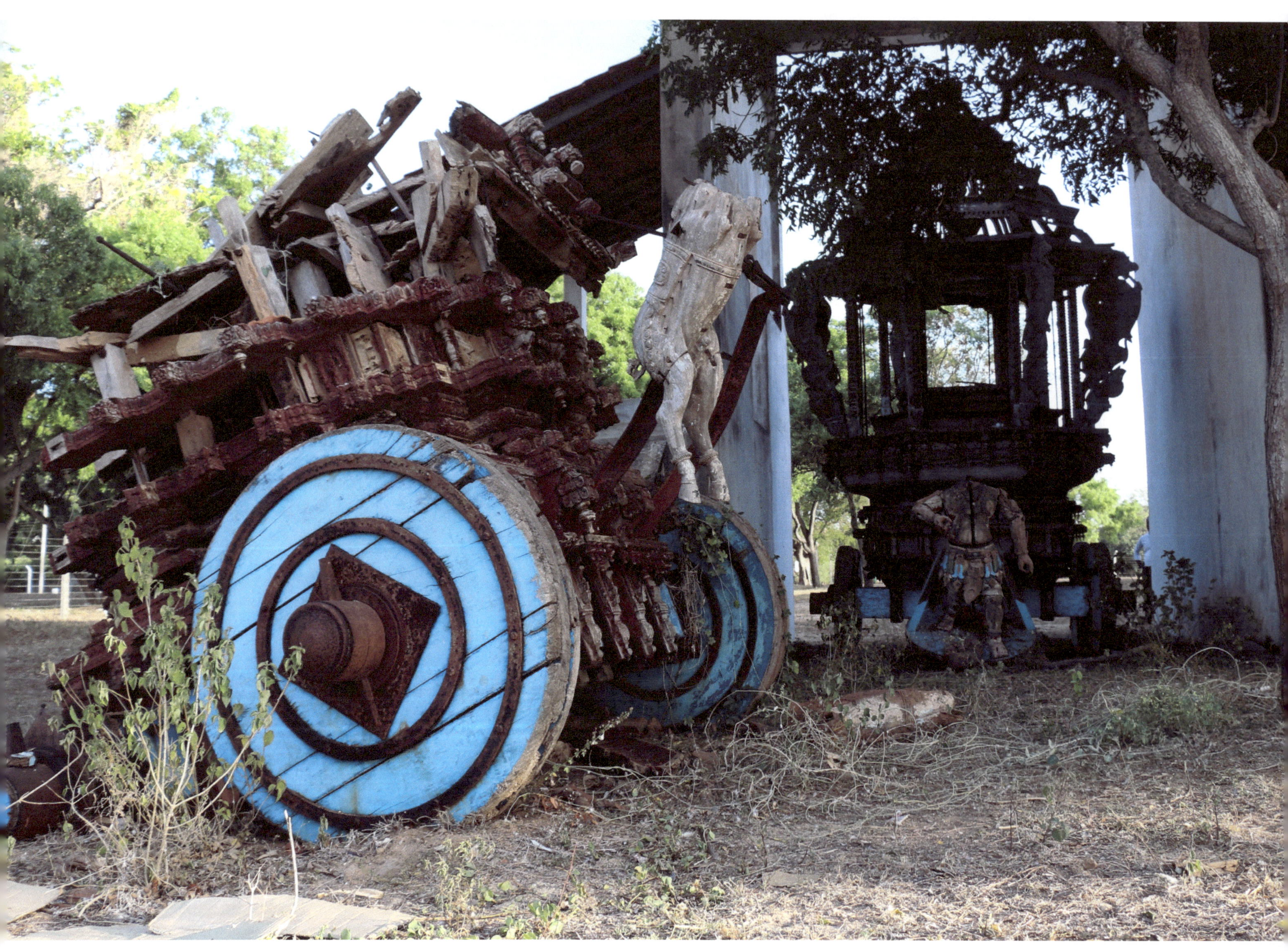

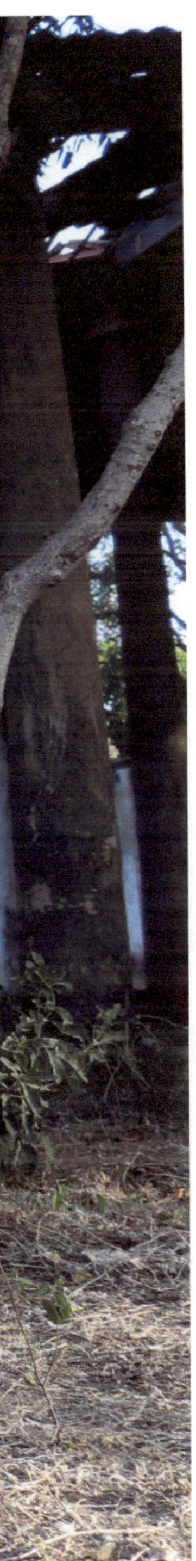

Wounds of the war

இலங்கையின் சிறுபான்மையினரின் ஒரு பகுதியினராகிய தமிழர்கள் மீதான அடக்குமுறைக்கு எதிராக பெரும்பான்மை சிங்கள அரசை எதிர்த்து வாதிட்ட தமிழர் தரப்பு அரசியல் தோற்றுப்போகவே; 1970 களின் இறுதிகளில் போராட்டக் குழுக்கள் அரசுக்கு எதிராக மும்மரமாக ஆயுதம் ஏந்தின. கிட்டத்தட்ட 30 ஆண்டுகளுக்கு மேலாக நீடித்த இந்த ஆயுதப் போராட்டம் பல எழுச்சியையும் வீழ்ச்சியையும் கண்டு இறுதியில் 2009 இல் சர்வதேச நாடுகளின் பேருதவியுடன் பெரும் இன அழிப்பு ஒன்றை ஆறாத சுவடாக்கி ஓய்ந்தது.

அந்த யுத்த குற்றப் பின்னணியை வைத்து சர்வதேசமே பெரும்பான்மை அரசுக்கு எதிராக சர்வதேச அளவிலான வழக்கை எடுத்துள்ள நிலையில்; அதன் எதிரொலியாக 1990 களில் அரசால் கைப்பற்றப்பட்ட தமிழ் மக்கள் வாழ்வாதார வளமான பிரதேசங்கள் மெல்ல மெல்ல தற்போது விடுவிக்கப்பட்டு வருகிறது. அப்படி விடுவிக்கப்பட்ட ஒரு மிக முக்கிய பிரதேசத்தின் ஒரு கோவில் சிதைவுதான் இந்தப் புகைப்படம். மயிலிட்டி துறைமுகத்தின் மிக அருகில் இருக்கும் பிரசித்தி பெற்ற கண்ணகி அம்மன் கோவிலின் பழமையான தேர் மற்றும் மஞ்சத்தின் சிதைவுகள்தான் அவை.

இலங்கையின் வடக்கின் கடல் வளத்தின் மிகச்சிறப்பான பகுதியாகச் சொல்லப்பட்ட; மிகப்பெரும் மீன் வளத்தைக் கொண்ட மயிலிட்டி துறைமுகம் விடுவிக்கப்பட்டது பெரும் மகிழ்ச்சியை அந்த பிரதேசம் சார்ந்த மக்களுக்கு ஏற்படுத்தியது. கிட்டத்தட்ட 27 ஆண்டுகளுக்கு பின்னர் தம் சொந்த மண்ணின் காற்றை அவர்கள் சுவாசித்தனர், தம் நிலங்களை ஸ்பரிச்சித்தனர், அது ஒரு பேருணர்வு.

27 ஆண்டுகளுக்கு முன்னர் இரண்டு வயதில் அந்த இடத்தை விட்டு பிரிந்தவர்கள்; இரண்டு குழந்தைகளை பெற்ற பின்னர் தம் மண்ணில் கால் பதித்திருந்தனர். தம் மண்ணை தாயைப்போல நேசித்த, தம் மண்ணில் இறுதிவரை கால் வைக்க முடியாமல் மரணித்தவர்கள் ஆன்மாக்களும் அன்றுதான் சாந்தியடைந்திருக்கும். இன்னமும் வெளிநாடுகளில் தஞ்சம் அடைந்தவர்களும் தம் மண்ணின் ஸ்பரிசத்திற்க்கான நாட்களை எப்போதென்று எதிர் பார்த்துக் காத்திருக்கிறார்கள்.

27 ஆண்டுகளுக்கு முன்னர் பெரும் மக்கள் வெள்ளத்தில் தேர் வீதியுலா வந்த நினைவுகளுடன் இருப்பவர்களுக்கு ; இன்றைய சிதைந்து போயுள்ள நிலையிலிருக்கும் தேரின் காட்சி மனதில் வலியையும் ஏதோ ஒரு பேரிழப்பையும், அதே நேரம் பசுமையான பழைய ஞாபகத்தையும் மீட்டிச்செல்லும். இன்று மீண்டும் அந்த இடம் கிடைத்திருக்கிறது, மீண்டும் கோவிலும் தேரும் புணரூத்தாபனம் செய்யப்பட்டுவிடும், ஆனால் அன்றிருந்த மக்கள் வெள்ளம்? அது திரும்ப வருமா?

சொந்த ஊரை விட்டு, நாட்டை விட்டு எங்கெங்கோ பிரிந்திருக்கும் அல்லல்பட்ட, சபிக்கப்பட்ட எம் இனம் மீண்டும் தன் நிலத்தில் ஸ்திரமாக காலூன்றி தன் வரலாற்றை தாய் மண்ணில் எழுதுமா? தந்தையும் தாயும் தம்மை பரன் பரையாக்கி வேரூன்றி தாய் மண்ணில் தன் தலைமுறையை விருட்சமாக்குமா? எதிர்காலம் நல்லதைக் கொடுக்கவேண்டும்.

இன்னமும் விடுபடாமல் இருக்கும் பிரதேசங்களும் விடுவிக்கப்பட வேண்டும், மீண்டும் 1980 களுக்கு முன்னிருந்த இனப்பரம்பல், சந்தோசம், கொண்டாட்டம் சொந்த நிலங்களில் கோலோச்ச வேண்டும்; கல்வியும் வளங்களும் தலைமுறை கடந்து வழங்க வேண்டும், இவை நடக்கும். அதற்கு இந்த இழந்த, பறிக்கப்பட்ட, எடுக்கப்பட்ட எம் உணர்வுடன் கூடிய உடைமைகள் சுவடுகளாக ஆவணமாக்கப்படுத்தப்பட வேண்டும்....!

The Sri Lankan civil war started between the government and the rebels in the 1970s, when negotiations between the Sri Lankan government and the Tamil political parties failed to protect the rights of minority Tamil ethnic groups. After almost three decades of war and several uprisings and downfalls, the war ended with massive genocide with the assistance of the international community.

After the war the Sri Lankan Government were answerable to an international tribunal, and were forced to release land captured in the 1990s back to the Tamil people. This photograph was taken in one of those places. It shows ruined parts of a temple cart which belongs to a temple called Kannaki Amman situated in Mayilti, Jaffna.

The Mayilti harbour is a rich and well-known fishing resource. The release of the harbour back to the Tamil people was a cause for great celebration. They returned back to their birthplace after 27 years. They felt the soil and air as a gift after a long struggle.

Some people among the dwellers of that place had left when they were 2 years old and returned to their homeland as adults with families of their own. It meant that people who had struggled and rebelled for their own land and died, could peacefully go to heaven after these incidents. Even still, there are several people who live as refugees in other countries, still eagerly waiting to return to their home land.

The ruins of the Temple cart are a source of pain for the people who saw the cart roaming around the temple in the middle of the crowd 27 years ago. It also reminds them of the wounds of the war and the old bitter memories. After 27 years we will be able to renovate the place, we can renovate the temple and the temple cart, but are we able to bring back the people?

 Are the People who migrated during the course of the war, able to resettle with peace in reconciliation in their home land? Are they able to build future generations with harmony?

In order to achieve this, the places that are still under government control should be released completely. People should be able to follow their traditional celebrations and festivals in the same manner which existed 30years ago. Education and all resources should be distributed equitably. Above all, we need to document the ruins of traditions, culture, structures and places of livelihood.

Story and Photography by Arulanantham Jeevatharshan
Translation by Krushanth Thanabalasingam
Sri Lanka

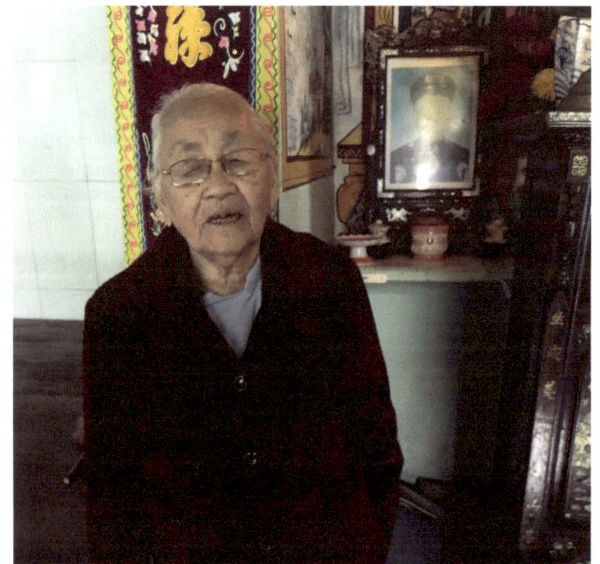

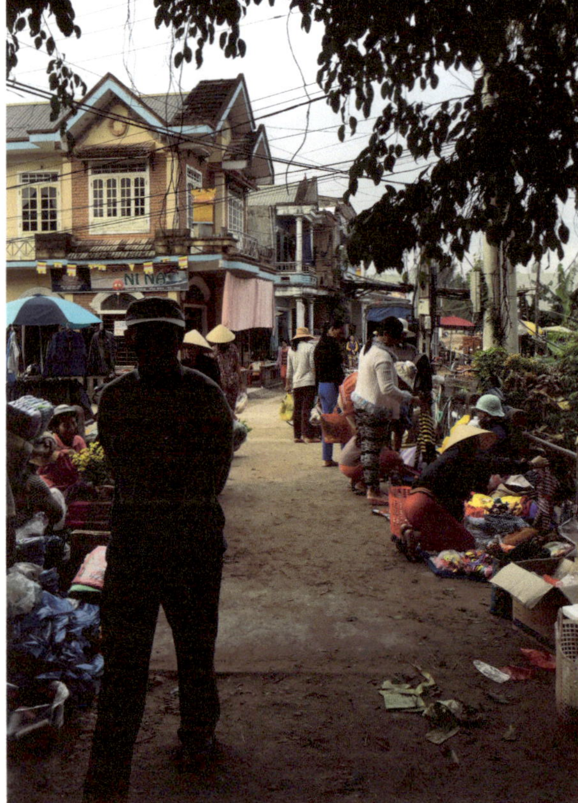

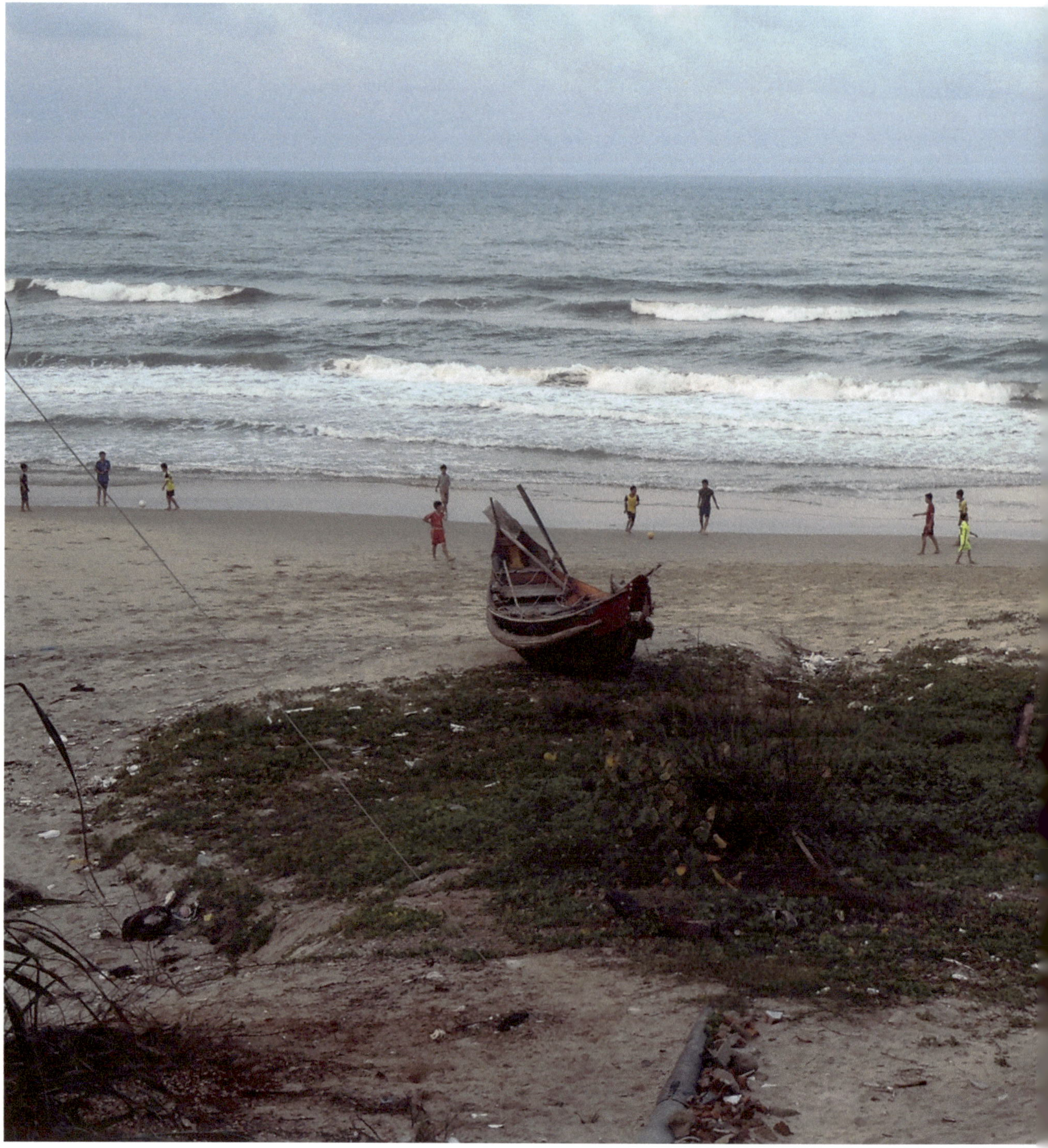

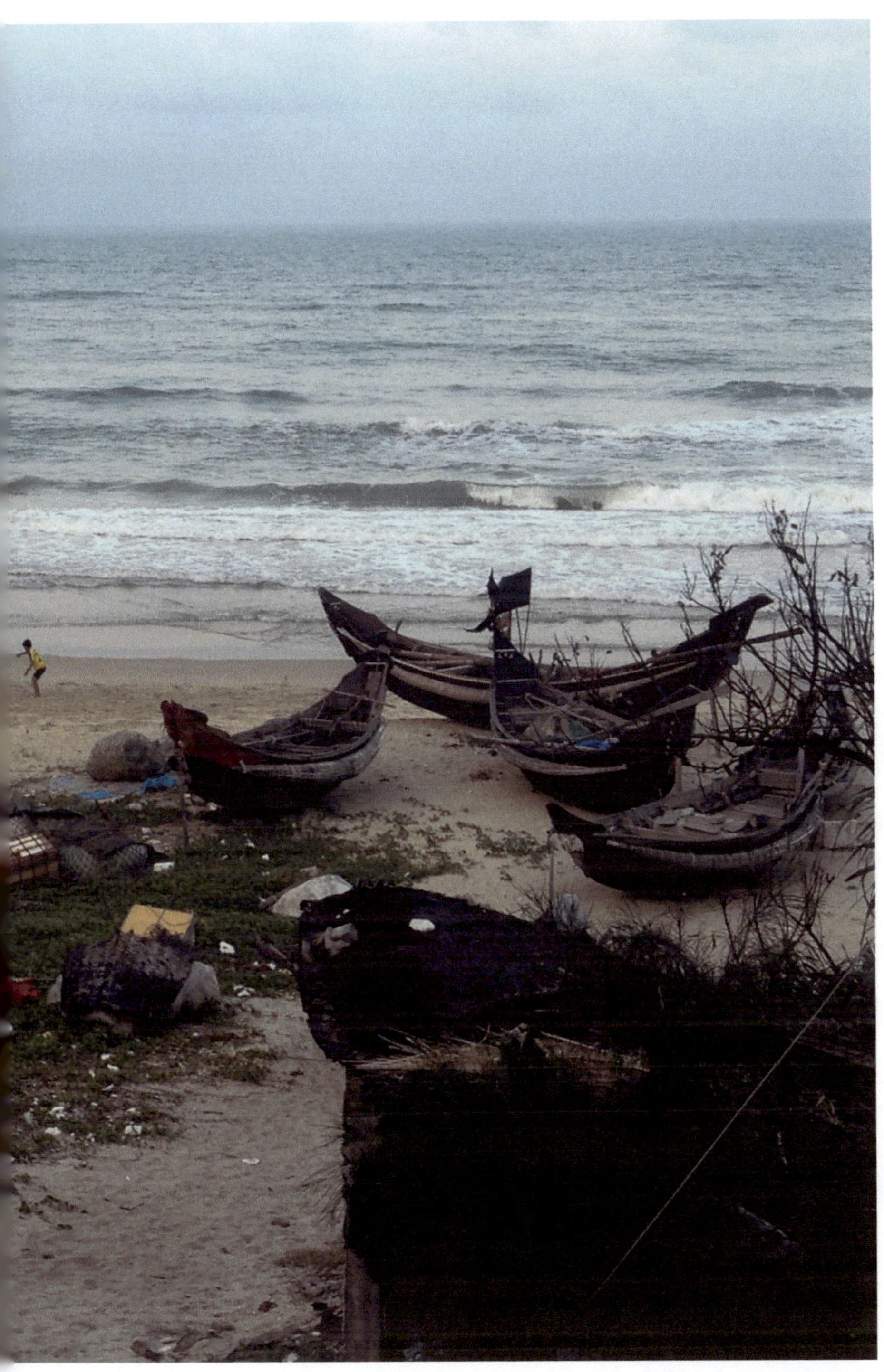

The cultural heart of Hue City

Trái tim văn hoá của thành phố Huế Tôi lớn lên ở một thành phố lịch sử ở miền Trung Việt Nam gọi là Huế. Tôi là một trong 10 anh chị em, vì vậy lớn lên tôi luôn bị bao vây bởi tình yêu, tiếng cười và sự hỗ trợ và học hỏi từ những điều tốt nhất. Khi tôi lớn lên ở Huế, chúng tôi đã chống lại mùa đông dưới ô dù và ponchos và không phải đề cập đến rất nhiều trò chơi trong nhà cùng với sự lạnh. Chúng tôi sống trong một ngôi làng khá xa ở các vùng cao, nơi có sự tiếp cận với giao thông vận tải, tương tác xã hội và thực phẩm để nuôi dưỡng hạn chế. Chúng tôi đã tiếp cận hạn chế các dịch vụ tài chính cơ bản như tín dụng, tiết kiệm và nguồn lực sản xuất. Cơ sở hạ tầng ở nông thôn Việt Nam cho đến ngày nay còn nghèo hơn nhiều so với ở các thành phố. Nguồn cung cấp không đáng tin cậy và dịch vụ chăm sóc sức khoẻ vẫn còn hạn chế.

Tuy nhiên, học cách sống với ít hơn là một sự theo đuổi quan trọng từ kinh nghiệm của tôi trong những năm trước khi tôi trưởng thành. Nó dạy cho tôi giá trị của những điều ngay trước mặt tôi và cho phép tôi đánh giá cao họ nhiều hơn. Mẹ tôi là một trong hàng ngàn bà vợ Việt Nam đã từng sống sót sau cuộc chiến. Mặc dù có những sự kiện thảm khốc đã xảy ra trong quá khứ, cô vẫn vẫn hạnh phúc và hài lòng cho đến ngày nay.

I grew up in a historic imperial city in central Vietnam called Hue. I was one of 10 siblings, so growing up I was always surrounded by love, laughter and support and definitely learnt from the best. When I was growing up in Hue, we weathered the winter under umbrellas and ponchos, not to mention lots of indoor games, all bundled up against the chill. We lived in quite a remote village in highland areas, where there was limited access to transportation, social interaction and food for nourishment. We had limited access to basic financial services such as credit, savings and productive resources. Infrastructure in rural Vietnam till this day is much poorer than it is in the cities. Power supplies are quite unreliable and availability of health services is still quite limited.

However, learning how to live with less was an important pursuit from my experience in the years leading up to my adulthood. It taught me the value of the things right in front of me and allowed me to appreciate them even more. My mother was one of thousands of Vietnamese wives and mothers who bravely survived the war. Despite catastrophic events that have occurred in the past, she remains happy and content till this day.

Story by Nguyễn Ngọc Dũng
Photography & Translation by Johnny Nguyễn

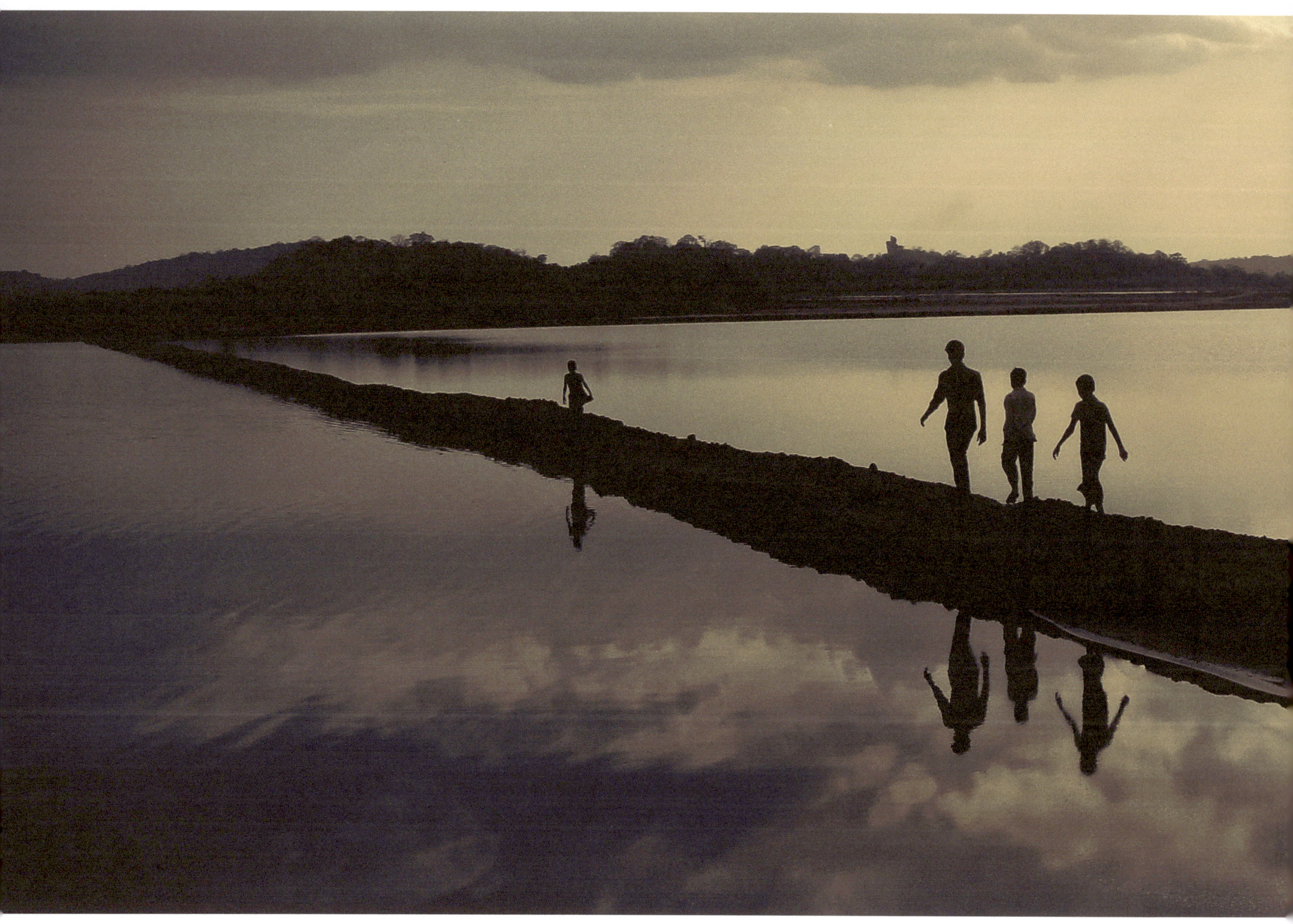

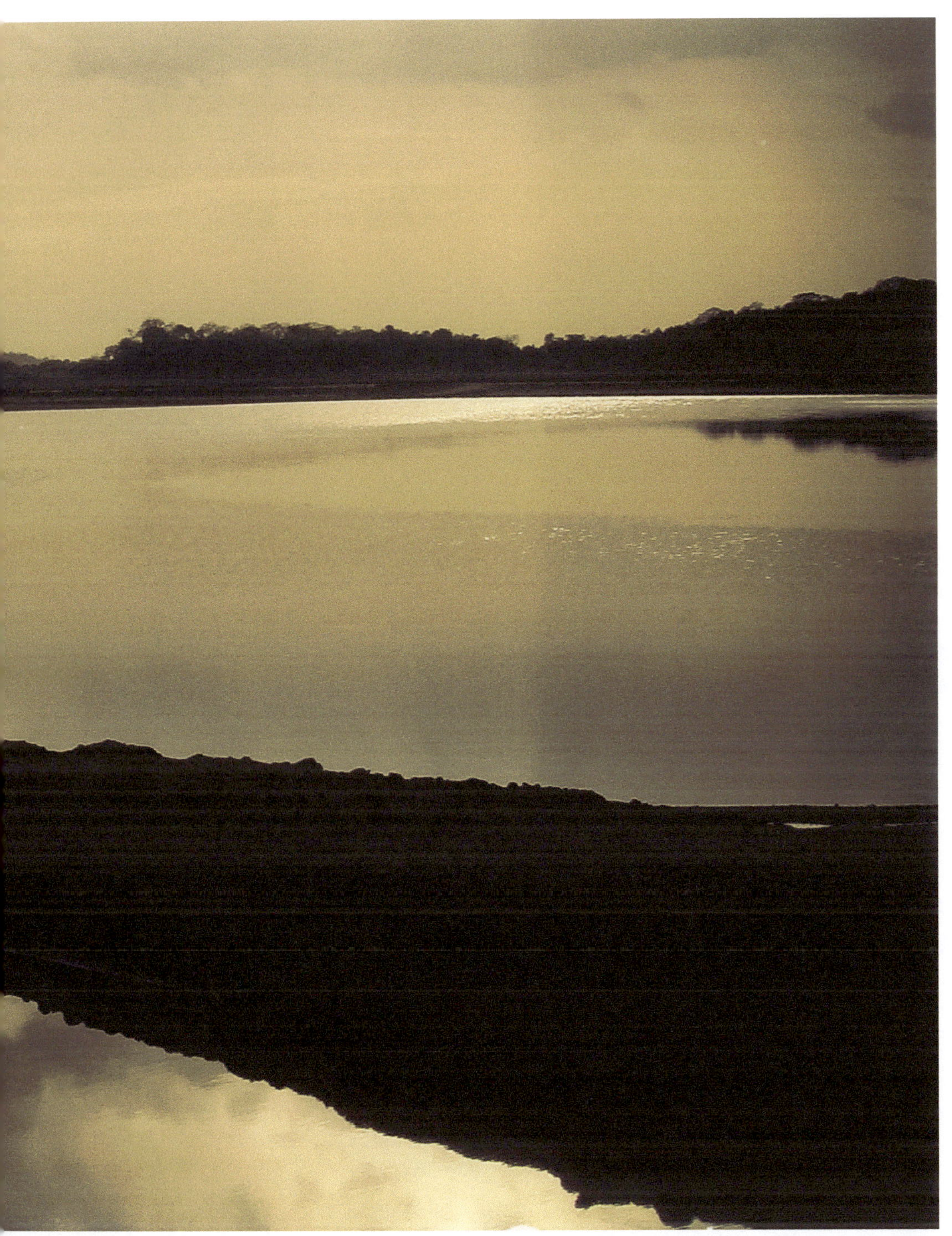

Seeds

இந்த புகைப்படமானது இலங்கையின் கிழக்குக்கரையோரத்தில் அமைந்துள்ள கிராமத்தில் எடுக்கப்பட்டதாகும். இக்கிராமத்தின் வாழ்வாதாரம் உப்பு உற்பத்தி, விவசாயம், விலங்கு வேளாண்மை மற்றும் மீன்பிடியில் தங்கியுள்ளது. இலங்கையின் இக்கிழக்கு பிரதேசமானது நீண்ட வரலாற்றையும் பாரம்பரியத்தையும் கொண்டுள்ளது இதற்கு சான்று அங்கு காணப்படும் கட்டிடங்களும் அமைப்புக்களும் ஆகும். நீண்டகால அசாதாரண சூழ்நிலையின் போது மக்கள் இடப்பெயர்வையும் பாரம்பரிய தொழிலையும் இழந்தனர் மீண்டும் இப்போதுதான் அவர்கள் வாழ்க்கை மீளக்கட்டியமைக்கபடுகின்றது.

இப்படத்திலே சிறுவர்கள் உப்பளம் வழியே உள்ள அணைக்கட்டுடாக நடந்து செல்வது போன்று அமைக்கப்பட்டிருக்கும் இதனூடே நான் உணர்த்த விளைவது நம் இறந்தகாலம், நிகழ்காலம் மற்றும் எதிர்காலம். சிறுவர்கள் நாளைய தலைவர்கள் அவர்களுக்கு நல்ஒழுக்கத்தை விதைப்பதன் மூலம் அவர்களை மட்டுமல்ல நாளைய சமுதாயத்தை கட்டியெழுப்ப முடியும்.

இந்த நல்விதைகள் தான் நாளை அவர்கள் சவால்களை வெற்றிகொள்ள உதவும், அத்தோடு நாம் கடந்தகால கசப்பான சம்பவங்களை மறந்து எதிர்கால சமாதானத்தையம் வளர்ச்சியையும் முன்னிறுத்தி இச்சிறுவர்கள் போல முன்னோக்கி நடக்கவேண்டும்.

This photograph was take in a remote village on the East Coast of Sri Lanka. The area is well known for salt cultivation, animal farming, fishing and rice. The eastern part of Sri Lanka has a long heritage of being a global marketplace and holds a lot of history that can be viewed through the structures around the city. During ethnics tensions in Sri Lanka, these people were dislocated from their land and their traditional livelihood and are now in the process of rebuilding their way of life.

This photograph shows children walking along the Dam wall where the salt is harvested. To me, this photo is symbolic of the way that the past, present and future interact. The division of water reminds us of when the war while the future of the children is reflected in the salt pools. It is important that we teach children to sow good seeds so that they can survive the new challenges that their world is facing and the next generation will have their future as clearly reflected as this.

All children are potentially the leaders of the future and hold the tools for peace and progress. So it is time to walk forward and not look back, as these children are doing.

Story and Photography by Krushanth Thanabalasingam
Sri Lanka

Niño the donkey

Había una vez un burro llamado "niño", el cual era muy tierno y juguetón y vivía en el Valle del Cócora, un paisaje natural localizado en un valle montañoso de la cordillera Central de los Andes colombianos. Niño era contemplado y acariciado por los turistas que diariamente visitaban el lugar, pues era un burro muy dulce. Pero un día, Niño se escapó de la granja en que vivía, su amo estaba muy preocupado, pues él y su esposa lo querían mucho. Inmediatamente avisaron a todas las personas del lugar para que estuvieran al pendiente del burro pero fue inútil, Niño no apareció.

Una semana después del suceso, un grupo de fotógrafos vino a tomar fotos en Salento y el Valle del Cócora. Mayra, una de las chicas que hacían parte de este grupo pudo apreciar a lo lejos entre las montañas lo que parecía un burro perdido. Inmediatamente llamó a sus compañeros y uno de ellos llamó a un capataz de una finca cercana, pues tal vez este podría ser su burro.

-¡Señor, señor! ¡Hay un burro perdido en las montañas! ¿No es suyo?- grito Juan, un chico del grupo de fotógrafos.

- ¡Es el burro de mi compadre Hernán! ¡Lo ha estado buscando como loco! – contestó el capataz efusivamente.

El capataz llamó rápidamente a Hernán y se dispusieron a ir por el burro. Niño estaba en una pequeña finca que estaba a 15 kilómetros de la finca de Hernán. Al llegar, un anciano robusto y bonachón los recibió con un ademan de bienvenida.

-¡Buenas!, el burro vino hasta acá buscando agua y todos estos días ha estado como angustiado. ¿Es de ustedes?- preguntó el hombre consternado.

¡Sí, es mi burro! ¡Muchas gracias por haberlo cuidado!-contestó Hernán muy emocionado.

Finalmente, Niño fue llevado de nuevo a su hogar y todos lo recibieron con una calurosa bienvenida. El grupo de fotógrafos seguía en el Valle del Cócora y Mayra, la chica que vio primero al burro decidió tomarle una foto para recordar siempre esa curiosa experiencia.

Once upon a time there was a donkey called "Niño". It was a very special and playful animal that lived in the Cocora Valley, a natural landscape, located in a mountainous area in Cordillera Central of the Andes of Colombia.

"Niño" was spoiled and cared for by the tourists who visited the place; they considered him a very sweet donkey. But, one day, "Niño" escaped from the farm where he lived. Its owners were very worried and concerned about his well- being. They immediately asked all the people of the Valley to help them to lookout for the donkey. However, it was useless, "Niño" did not appear.

A week after his disappearance, a group of photographers from another city went to the Cocora Valley to take photos of its landscape. One of the girls of the group, named Mayra, saw something in the distance, it was between the mountains and she thought that maybe this was the lost donkey. Immediately, she called one of her friends John who went to advise the foreman from a nearby farm that they had seen the missing animal.

"Mr,Mr! There is a donkey between the mountains, isn't yours?" said John.

"Oh, it's my friend's donkey. Hernan has been looking for it like crazy!" answered the foreman.

The foreman went quickly to his friend's house and told him where "Niño" was seen. They got ready and went to look. Niño was in a small farm 15 kilometres from his house, where he may have gone looking for water.

These past days the donkey had been clearly distressed. The owner of the farm, who was an old man said, "Is that yours?"

"Yes, it is mine!" Said, Hernan excited. Thank you for taking care of him!

Finally, "Niño" was taken back to his home and was received with a warm welcome from the community of the Valley and the group of photographers. Mayra decided to take a picture of the moment to remember it as a curious experience in her life.

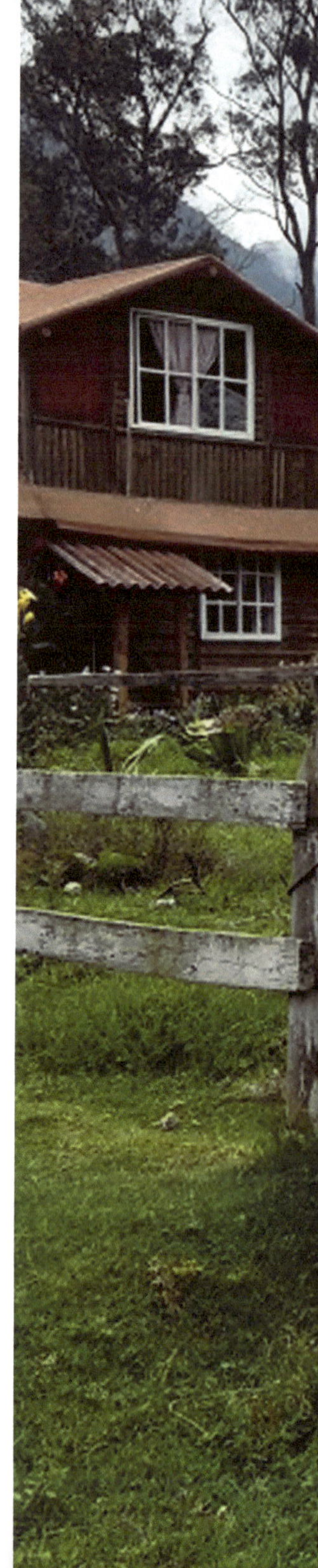

Story & Photography by Mayra Alejandra Abadia Quimbaya
Translation by Johana Bueno
Colombia

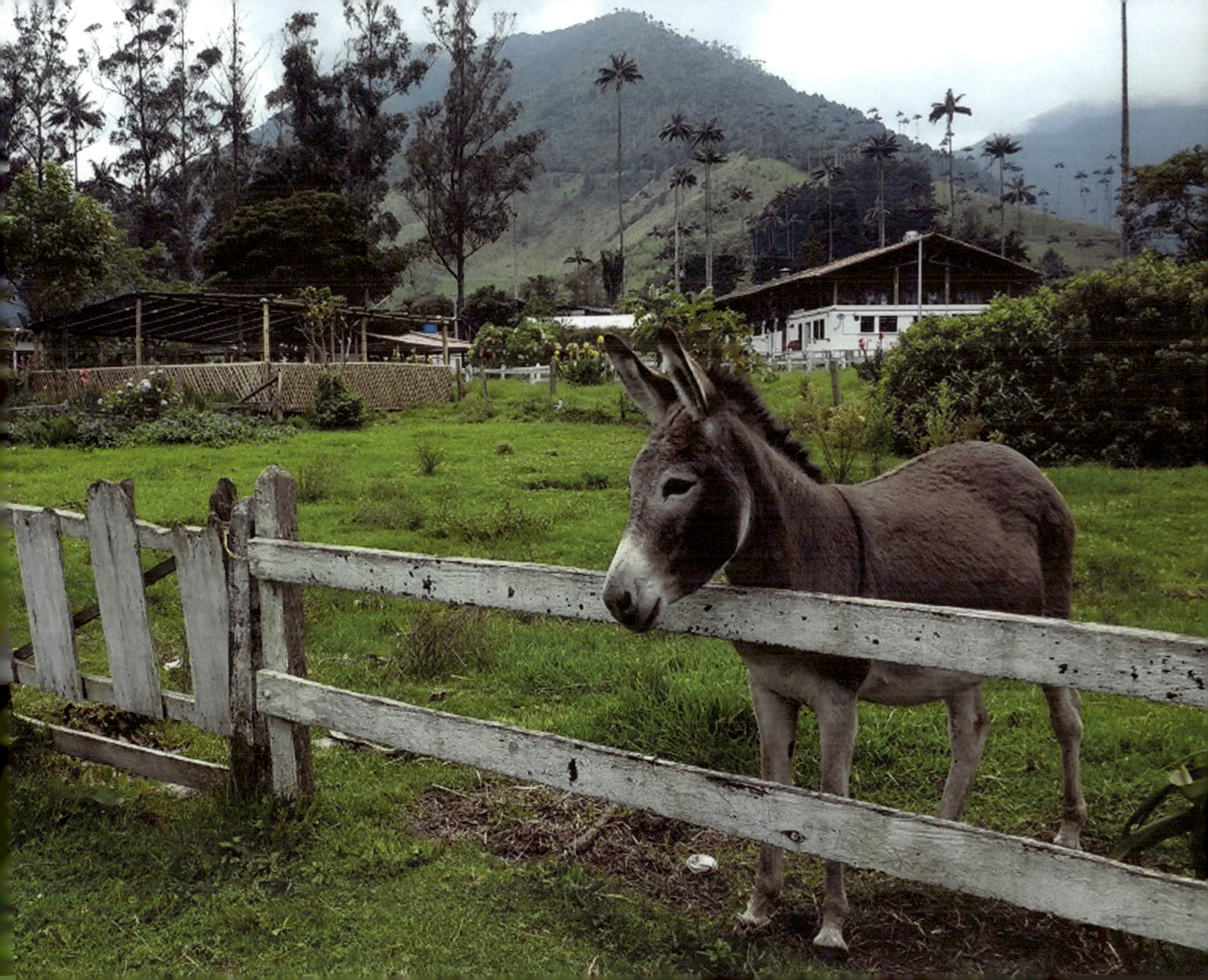

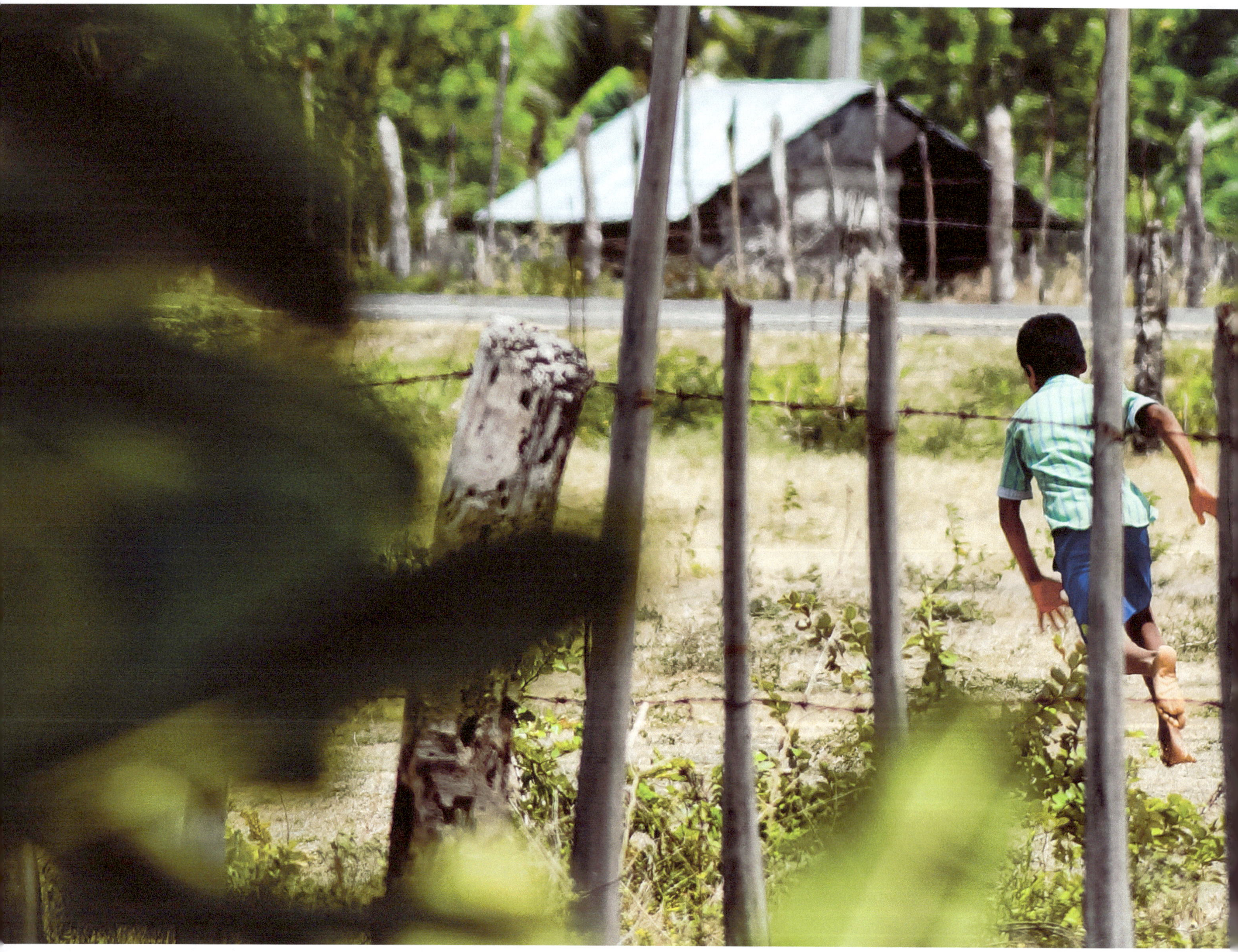

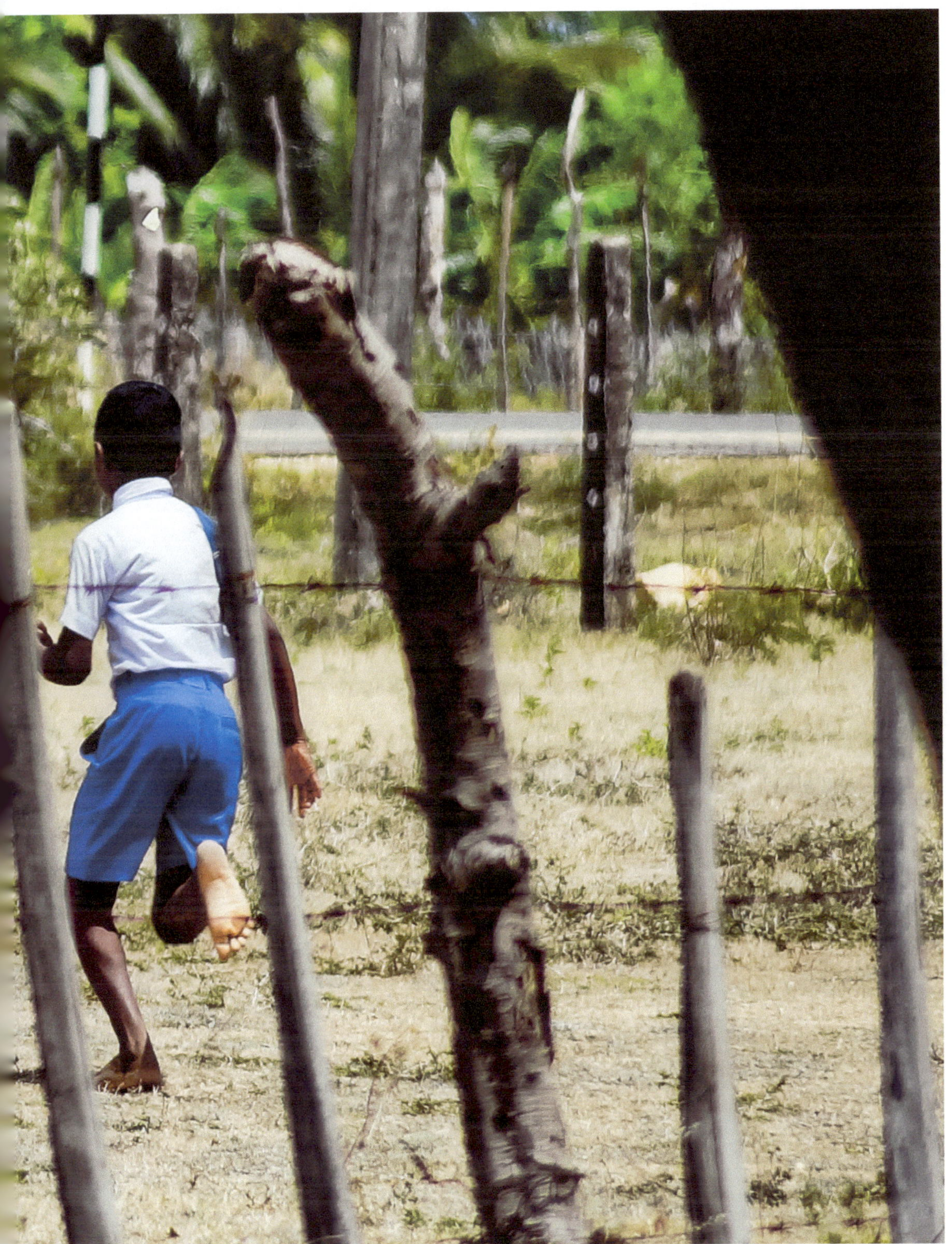

Tools for changing the world

இலங்கை இந்திய கடற்பரப்பில் அமைந்துள்ள உலகத்தில பழமையான வரலாற்றையும் பாரம்பரியத்தையும் கொண்டமைந்த ஒரு தீவாகும். இந்த பாரம்பரியமும் வரலாறாரும் ஒவ்வொரு சந்ததிகளாக புதுமைகளை ஏற்று பழமையை சிதைக்கா வண்ணம் பரிமாறப்பட்டு வரப்படுகிறது.

இலங்கை 1960 ஆண்டு இலவச கல்விக்கொள்கையை தழுவிக்கொண்டது, இதனூடாக ஏழை மக்களின் சமூக பொருளாதார மேம்பாடு வளர்ச்சி கண்டது. நல்ல கல்வி என்பது நாம் சுவாசிக்கும் சுத்தமான காற்றினைப்போல இன்றியமையாதது. எங்கள் பிள்ளைகளுக்கு கல்வி மறுக்க படுகின்ற போது, அது நாட்டின் சமூக பொருளாதார உறுதியினை குலைக்கும் அத்தோடு அடுத்து வரும் சந்ததியினையும் பாதிக்கும்.

இங்க காட்டப்படுகின்ற புகைப்படமானது இரு சிறார்கள் எதிர்திசையில் ஓடுவது போலவும் அதில் ஒருவன் பாடசாலை சீருடையோடும் மற்றையவர் சாதாரண ஆடையுடன் போடுவதாகவும் காட்டப்பட்டுள்ளது. இதன் அர்த்தம் கல்வி மறுக்கப்படுகின்ற நிலையில் சிறார்கள் வாழ்வின் எதிர்திசைக்கு தலைப்படுவதாகவும் இது அவர்களின் சமூக பொருளாதார நிலையினை பாதிப்பதோடு மட்டுமல்லாது சமூகத்தினையும் எதிர்கால சந்ததிகளையும் பாதிப்பதாக குறிக்கின்றது.

ஒரு நாட்டின் வளர்ச்சிக்கு கல்வி இன்றியமையாதது, அது எந்தவித பாகுபாடும் இன்றி சகலருக்கும் சமஉரித்துடன் பகிர்ந்தளிக்கப்படவேண்டும்.

As a tiny island in the Indian Ocean, Sri Lanka is enshrined in the heritage and customs of one of the oldest living cultures in the world today. This incredible history must be past down from one generation to the next through a combination of teaching both the old traditions and the new structures without allowing one to restrict the other.   Sri Lanka embraced a free education system in the late 1960's to enable social and economic mobility for the poorest people by increasing their ability to earn a living.

A good holistic education is as important as the air we breathe. When our children are denied an education it not only affects them as individuals but it also affects their communities and the social and economic structure of the country for generations to come. If you look closely and dissect this photograph it depicts two children running in opposite directions. One child is wearing a school uniform and the other is not. The aim of the photographer is to explore the different directions they could be taking in their lives.

The photograph represents a crossroads at which decisions are made that will have a profound effect on future outcomes and continue on as a ripple effect onto the descendants of our nation and our world. It is vital then for a country which has such an incredible heritage to preserve to make sure that education remains the focus to ensure that class does not stand in the way of equity.

Story & Photography by Krushanth Thanabalasingam
Sri Lanka

Old school cooking

In growing up, the smell of fresh Fijian and Indian sweets and cuisines was pretty much a common occurrence. Especially during Eid al Fitr, a time of celebration to mark the end of Ramadan (a holy month of fasting by Muslims).

A traditional dish served on Eid in our home is called Samai. Its a dish of fine, sweet noodles cooked in milk, spices, almonds and sultanas. It is tradition to offer this to guests on Eid day. I have great memories of cooking and making homemade Samai with my grandmother, my mum and my family. The smell of dough, the flour in the air, ghee and oil on the tables, it was heaven for a kid like me who loved play dough!

It was alot of hard work but my grandmother was the queen of old school cooking. Everything was done by memory, from scratch and with no recipes. For me, many of my most meaningful old family traditions and memories revolve around food with recipes passed down or specific family members preparing their specialties year after year.

Although we can get everything premade in packets now, somehow I find it quiet calming watching my mother cook from scratch using the old methods my grandmother used. Doing those things my grandmother use to do again and again at the same time and in the same way with the same people. Sometimes not even knowing why, but we just do it because any other way just doesn't feel right.

These pictures are from one of the last years that we made the Samai together. I remember sitting down and looking over at my grandmother and I realized she was so tired. Not from the work she has done that day, but from all the work that she had done in her 90 something years of existence. I made a commitment then that I would work hard learning how to cook for my family the way my mother learnt off her. I still have a long way to go.

Story & Photography by Shabnaaz Sheik Ahmed
Australia

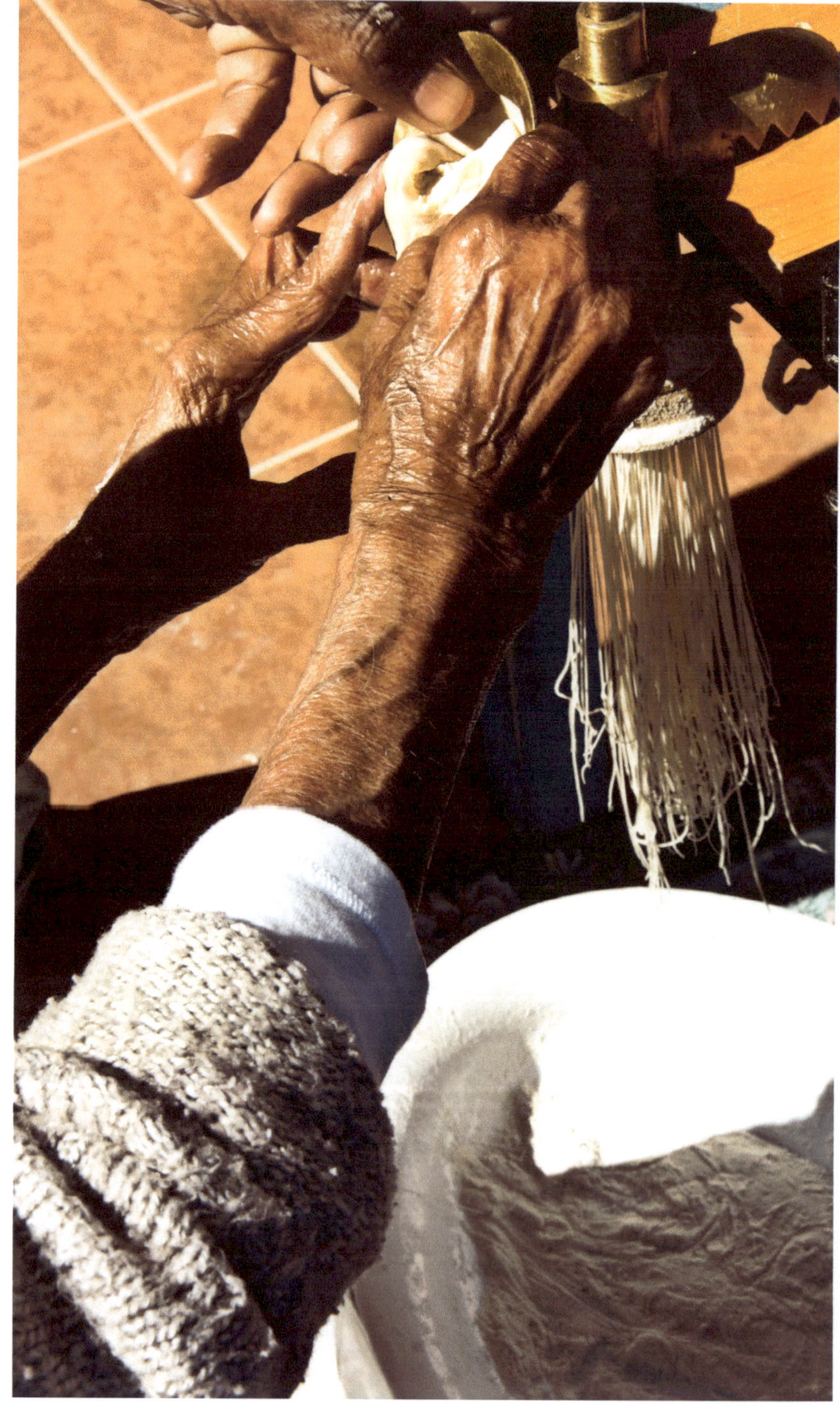

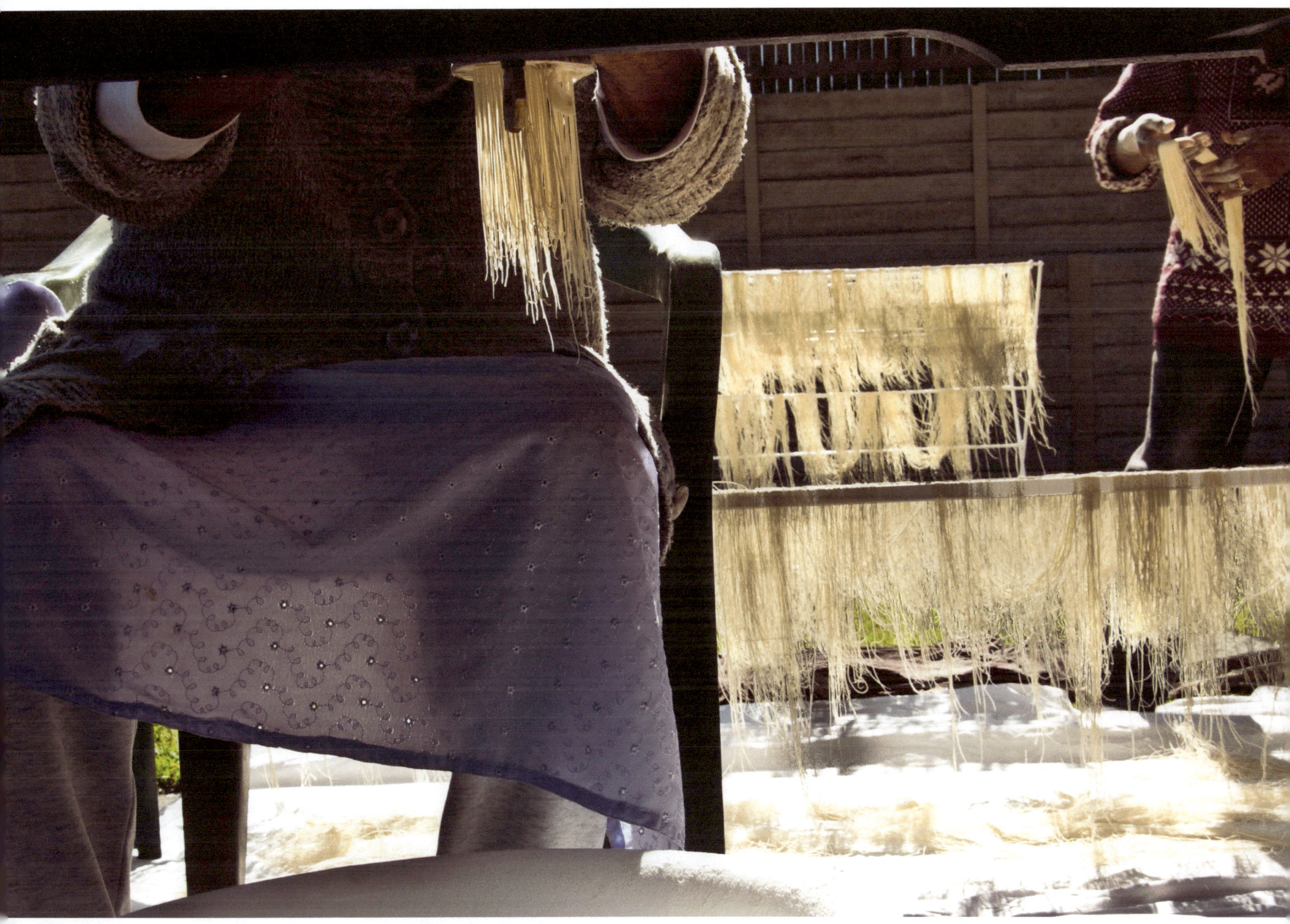

Icon of lost humanity

இந்த புகைப்படம் இலங்கையின் வடக்கு கரையோரத்தில் அமைந்துள்ள
முல்லைத்தீவு பிரதேசத்தில் எடுக்கப்பட்ட படமாகும். இந்த படத்தில் உள்ள
கப்பல் இக்கட்டான தருணத்தில் அல்லலுற்று அவதிப்பட்ட மக்களுக்கு
உதவிகளை சுமந்து வந்த சமயத்தில் கடலில் தரை தட்டி படத்தில் உள்ளவாறு
காணப்படுகிறது. இது கடந்தகாலம் மக்கள் பட்ட துன்பங்களையும்

துயர்களையும் சவால்களையும் தாங்கி நிற்கும் ஒரு நினைவுச்சின்னம். இந்த
கப்பல் பல அட்டூழியங்கள் அழிவுகள் என்பதை சாட்சியான போதும் எந்தவித
தீர்ப்பு வழங்க இயலவில்லை. கடந்தகால ஆயுத போராட்ட வடுக்களை சுமந்த
வண்ணம் தன்னுள் சோகங்களையும் இழைக்கப்பட்ட மனிதத்தினையும் சுமந்து
காட்சிதரும் ஒரு மீள் கட்டியமைக்கப்படும் தேசத்தின் நினைவுச்சின்னம்.

This photo was taken on the North Coast of Sri Lanka near Mullaitheevu.
The ship was intended to bring much needed aide to people who had
known hardship for much too long. Unfortunately, it did not reach its
destination safely and washed up on these beaches where it stands
now. It is a reminder of a period when the country was facing its biggest
challenges.

In its time the remains of this ship stood witness to many atrocities,
unable to condemn or pass judgement. It stood strong in the aftermath,
under the weight of sorrow that hung in the air as the people picked
their way through their lost humanity and today it stands tall to witness
the rebuilding of a nation. The shipwreck is one of many ruinous icons in
a country steeped in military history.

Story and Photography by Donbosco Prashanth
Translation by Krushanth Thanabalasingam
Sri lanka

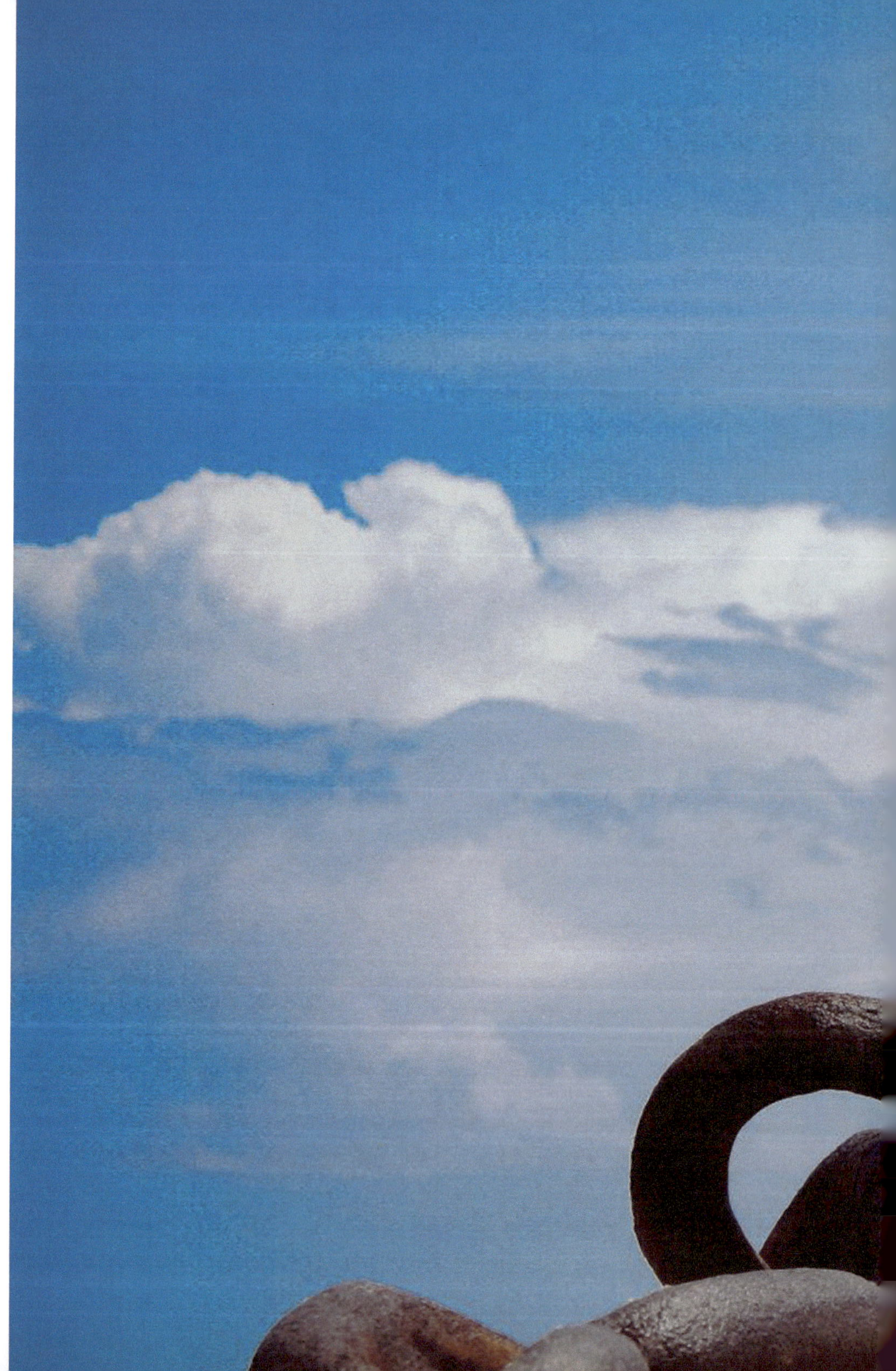

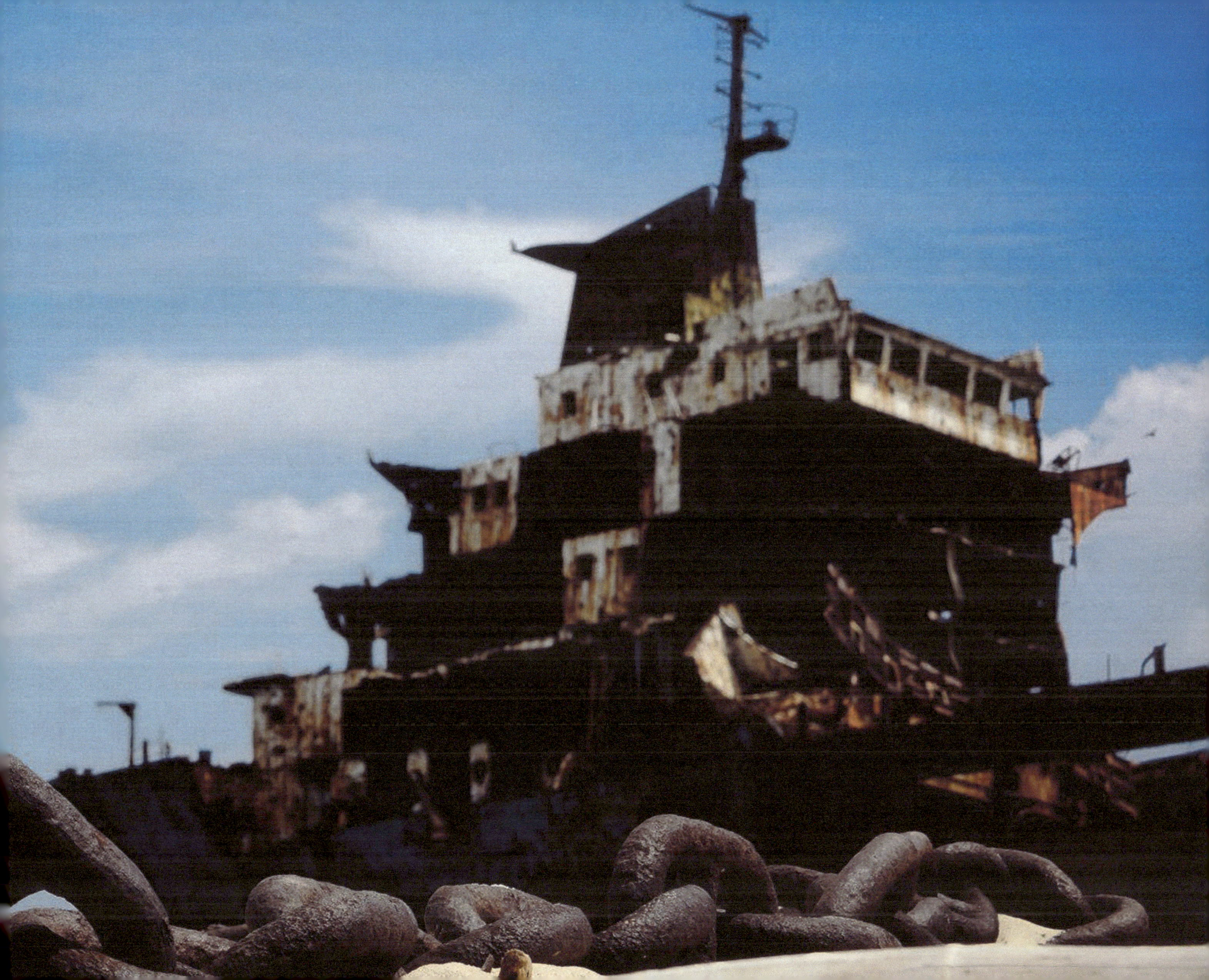

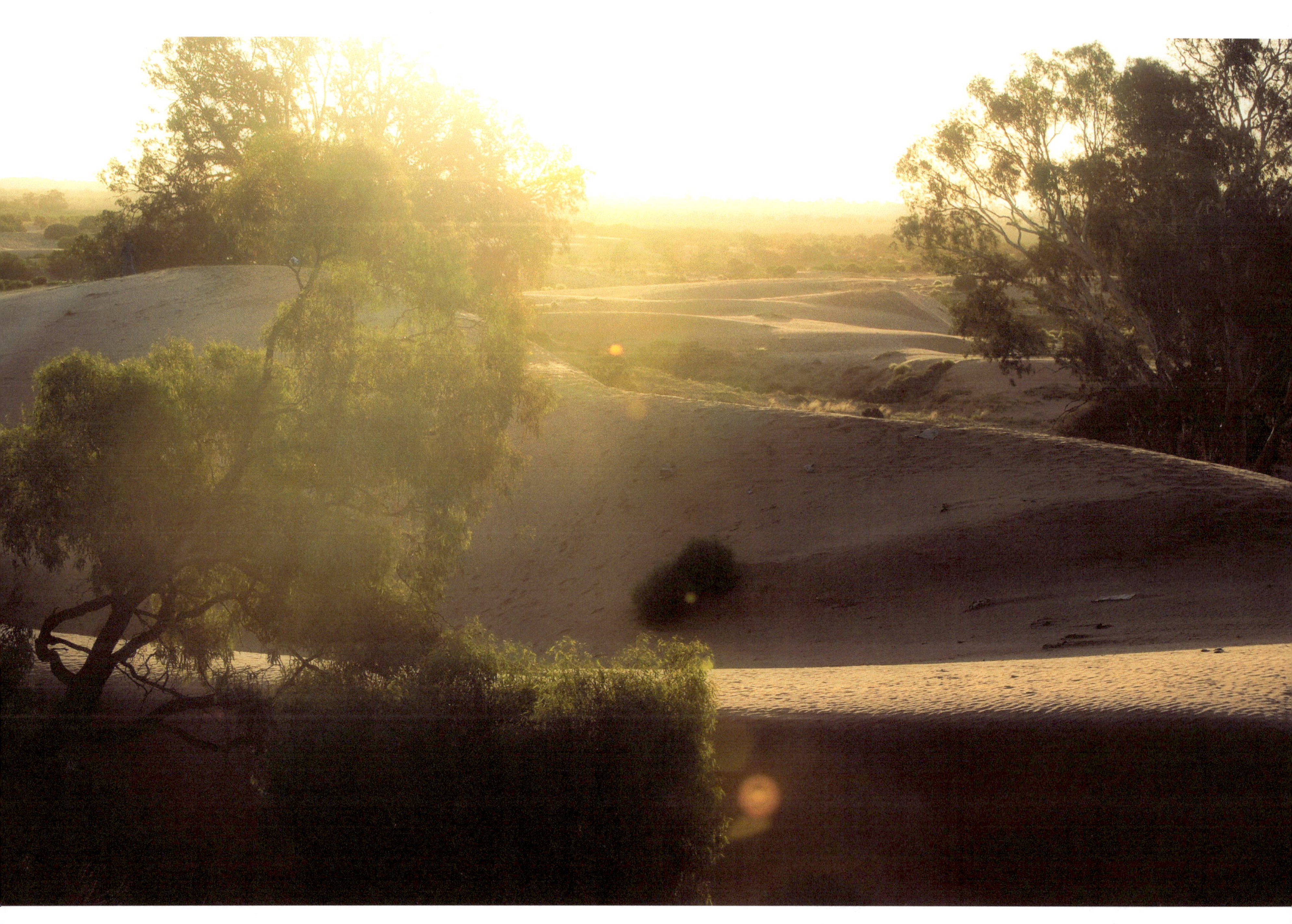

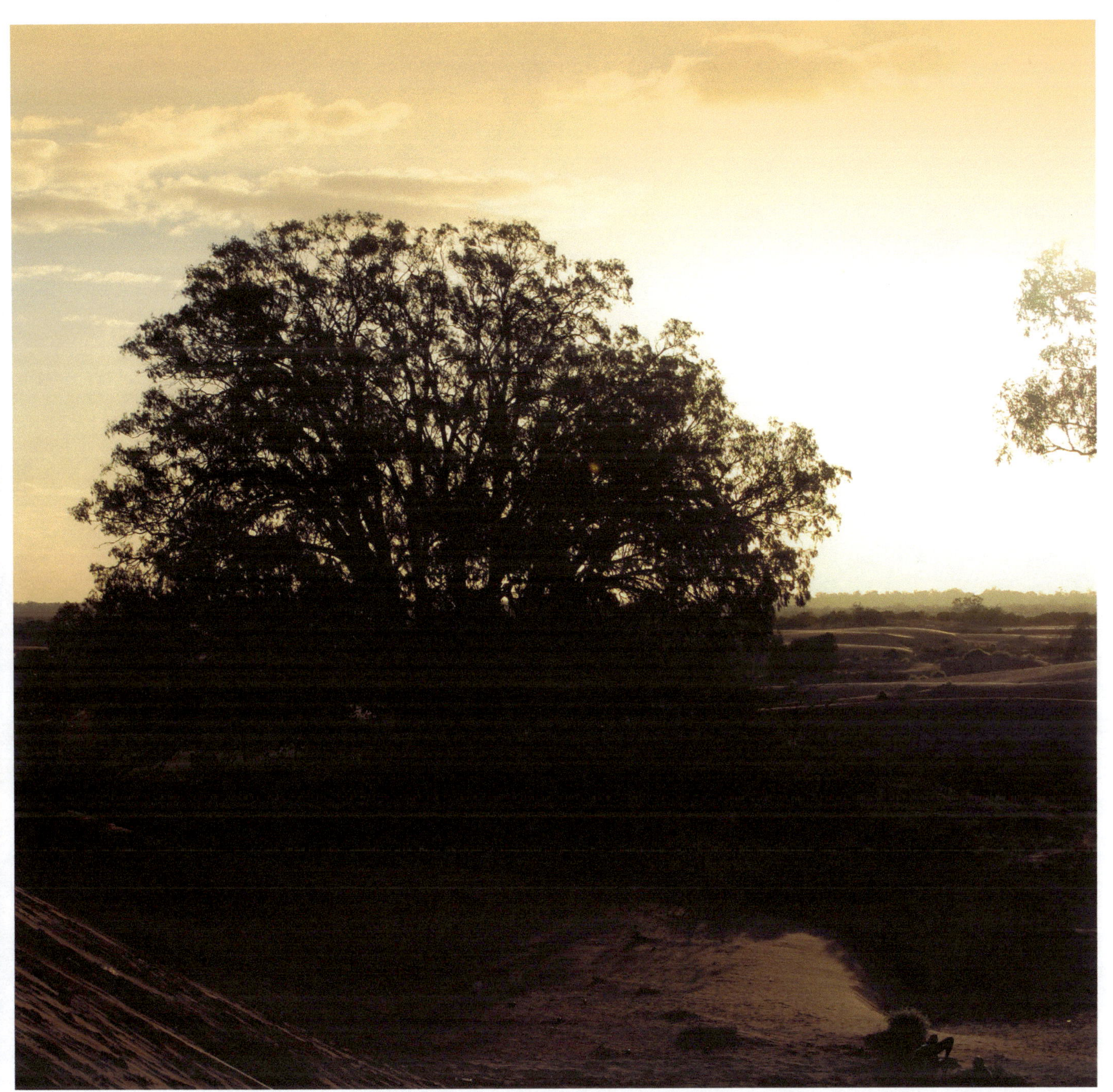

Details

Having had bad eyesight most of my life, I lived my life in blocks of colour and vague shapes. Details were something I never knew existed. I thought this was normal and learned to navigate through the world in other ways. It never occurred to me that this was not the way other people lived.

I got my first pair of glasses when I was ten. Suddenly the world was in focus and details were easy to spot from a distance and my world became a little less scary and so much bigger than the very small distance I could once only see. I found myself reveling in the tiny details I could never quite see and would spend hours looking at the tiny details, the lines, the cracks and the veins, tracing them in my mind, remembering them in case they were lost to me again.

Now, I take photos to capture the wonder and the details that still bring me so much joy and my hope is that others will be able to see the beauty I see in the world when the light touches the earth in that perfect little moment of synchronicity and the details emerge.

Photography & story by Atiya Karimshah
Australia

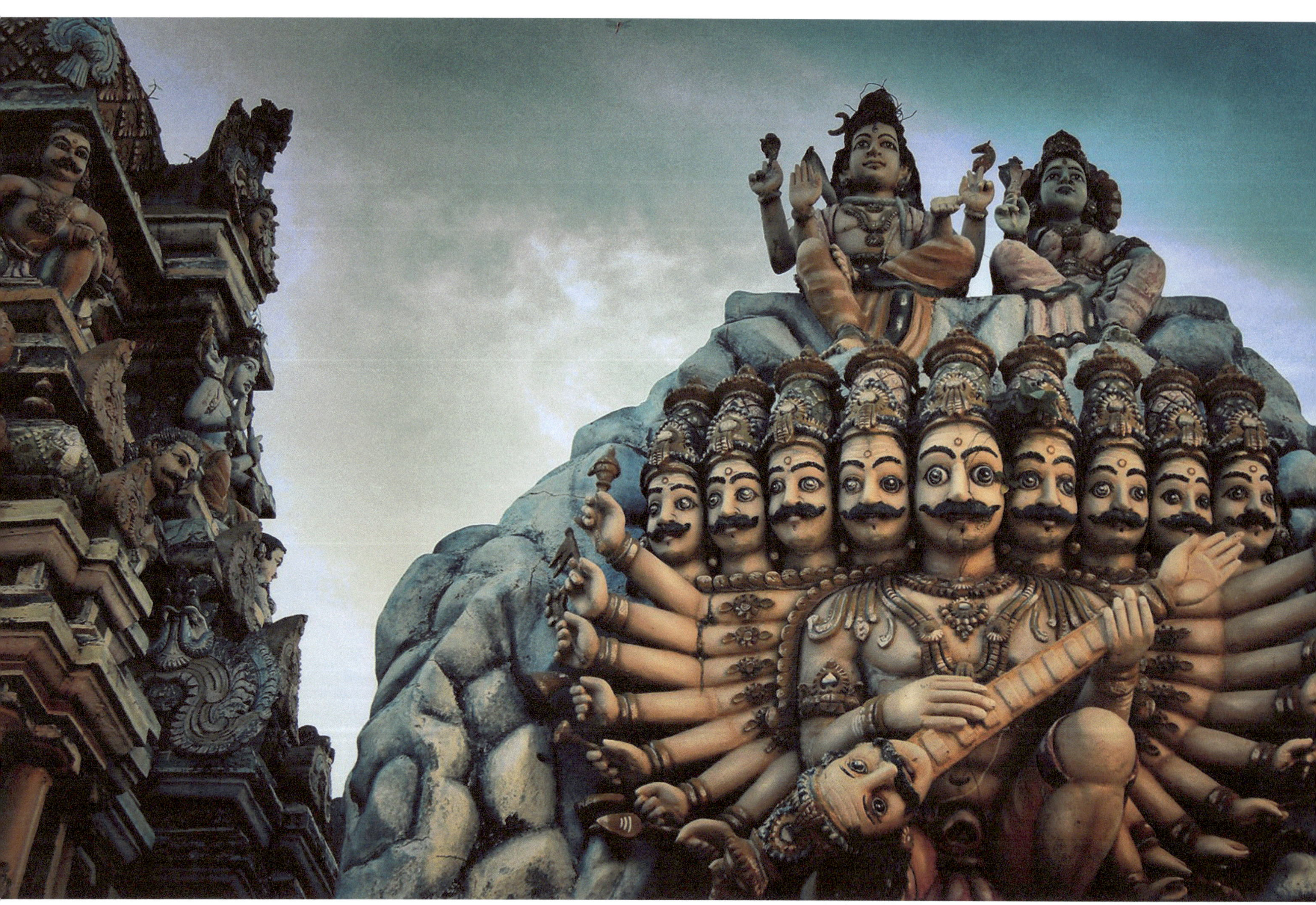

King Ravanan

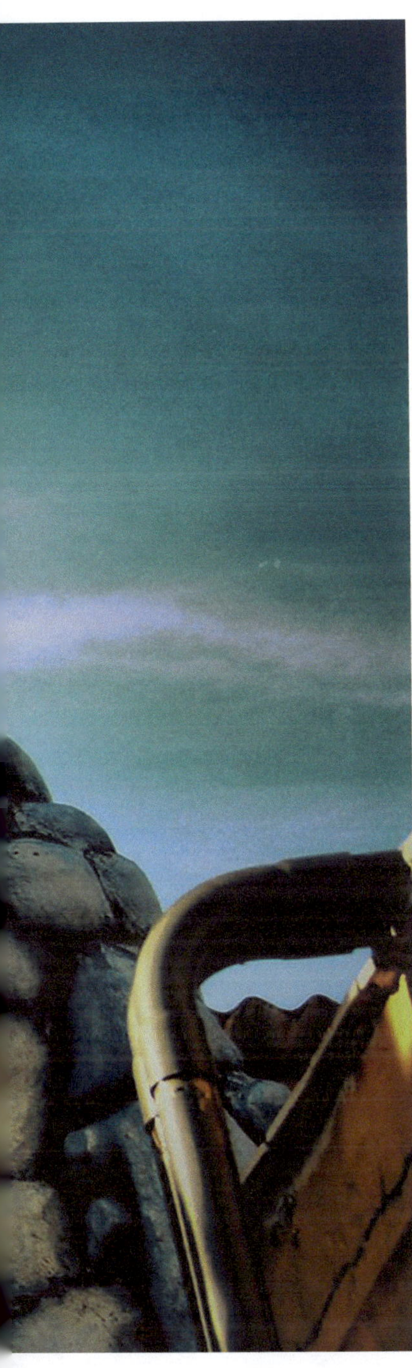

மன்னன் இராவணன் இலங்காபுரியினை (இலங்கை) அரச தர்ம நெறிகள் தவறாமல் ஆட்சி புரிந்து வந்தவன். இவன் பல கலைகளையும் கற்று அறிவிலும் தசாவதானியாகவும் சிறந்து விளங்கினான். இதன் விளைவாக இராவணனின் சிலை பத்து தலைகளை கொண்ட உருவமாக படைக்கப்பட்டுள்ளது, மேலும் இது இராவணன் 4 வேதங்களும் 6 சாஸ்திரங்களும் கற்றுணர்ந்ததை குறிப்பதாகவும் கூறுகின்றது. இங்கே பத்து தலைகள் என்பது பத்து துறைகளில் தலைசிறந்தவனாக இராவணன் இருந்தான் என்பதுவாகும். சிறந்த வீணை வித்துவான், சிறந்த சிவபக்தன், சிறந்த போராட்டல் கொண்ட வீரன் போன்ற பத்து குணாதிசயசிங்கள் கொண்டவனாகவும் கருதுகோள்கள் உள்ளன.

இராவணனை பற்றிய குறிப்புகள் பரவலாக பௌத்த, தாய்லாந்து, பர்மீய மற்றும் ஜெயின் கலாச்சாரங்களிலும் காணப்படுகின்றது. இதில் சிறிய வேறுபாடுகளும் காணப்படுகின்றது. இராவணன் 64 ஆய கலைகளும் கற்று தேர்ந்தவனாகவும் அனைத்து யுத்த கலைகளும் கற்றவனாகவும் சித்த வைத்தியம், வான சாஸ்திரம் போன்ற நூல்களை எழுதியவனும் ஆவான். அத்தோடு உலகின் முதலாவது பறக்கும் இயந்திரத்தை புஸ்பக விமானத்தை வடிவமைத்தது இவன் என்று வரலாறு கூறுகின்றது.

திருகோணமலையில் காணப்படுகின்ற கன்னியா வெந்நீர் கிணறு இவனின் வரலாற்றை குறிக்கும் நிகழ்கால சான்றாகும். இந்த கிணறுகள் இராவணனின் தாயின் மரண கிரியைகளை நாடாத்த அவனின் வாள் மூலம் பூமியின் 7 இடங்களில் துளையிடப்பட்ட வெந்நீர் ஊற்று கிணறுகளாகும். இன்றும் இந்துக்களின் மத வழிபாட்டு தலமகா இயற்கை ஊற்றாக காணப்படுகின்றது.

King Ravanan is said to have lived in ancient Lankapuri (modern day Sri Lanka). Not only was he known as a great champion of democracy and civil rights but he was also revered as the most intelligent person of his time and a great multitasker. This is reflected in the imagery of King Ravanan found in art, literature and sculptures as a man with 10 heads and 20 hands.

It is believed that Ravanan's 10 heads symbolize the 6 Shastra's and 4 Veda's (the 10 Hindu religious books). Some versions of his story depict him as actually having 10 heads which he progressively lost through annual sacrifices to his God, Shiva as a monument of his devotion until he was left with only one. The final head was considered the true head of Ravana and Shiva was appeased.

While there are many monuments to King Ravanan in his birth place, Sri Lanka the mythology of his existence has permeated borders and his likeness can be found in Buddhist, Thai, Burmese and Jain culture. Although their stories vary slightly Ravanan is magnanimous in his knowledge and spirituality wherever his story is told. He was known to be a great scholar of these and a master of 64 types of knowledge and all arts of weaponry. He was the author of the Ravana Samhita, a book of Hindu astrology and of the Arka Prakasham, a book of ancient medicines. Some even say that he was the inventor of the first flying machine called pushpaga vimaanam.

The Kanniya hot water springs in Trincomalee Sri Lanka are a living testament to King Ravanan's story. It is said that in preparation for his mother's funeral, King Ravanan struck the earth with his sword in seven spots and hot springs appeared at each point. The water in these wells continue to flow till this day and the springs are the site of many religious Hindu rituals dedicated to loved ones lost.

Story and Photography by: Donbosco Prashanth
Translation by : Krushanth Thanabalasingam
Sri Lanka

The power of coffee

The picture "Coffee" is taken in Australia in 2010. It looks strangely staged, but is not. The photographer does not know whether someone had left their coffees in favour of something much more interesting or the order had come to the wrong table. The seagulls were happy nevertheless.

The photographer thinks it is only fitting to feature a picture of coffee in a "coffee table" book, but it also serves a different purpose. The world we live in is diverse and despite the differences between us there are always reasons to connect. Something as simple as having a coffee can be the excuse needed to start a conversation. It can be the beginning of a new friendship, or a relationship. It can be a break you needed from studying or the energy boost for a productive work meeting. It can be the way you connect with someone who speaks a different language, or a token to show appreciation, or to comfort someone.

Coffee has an important function in many parts of the world and it is one of the things that connect us. One should not underestimate the power of coffee.

Photography by: Trine Vik
Australia

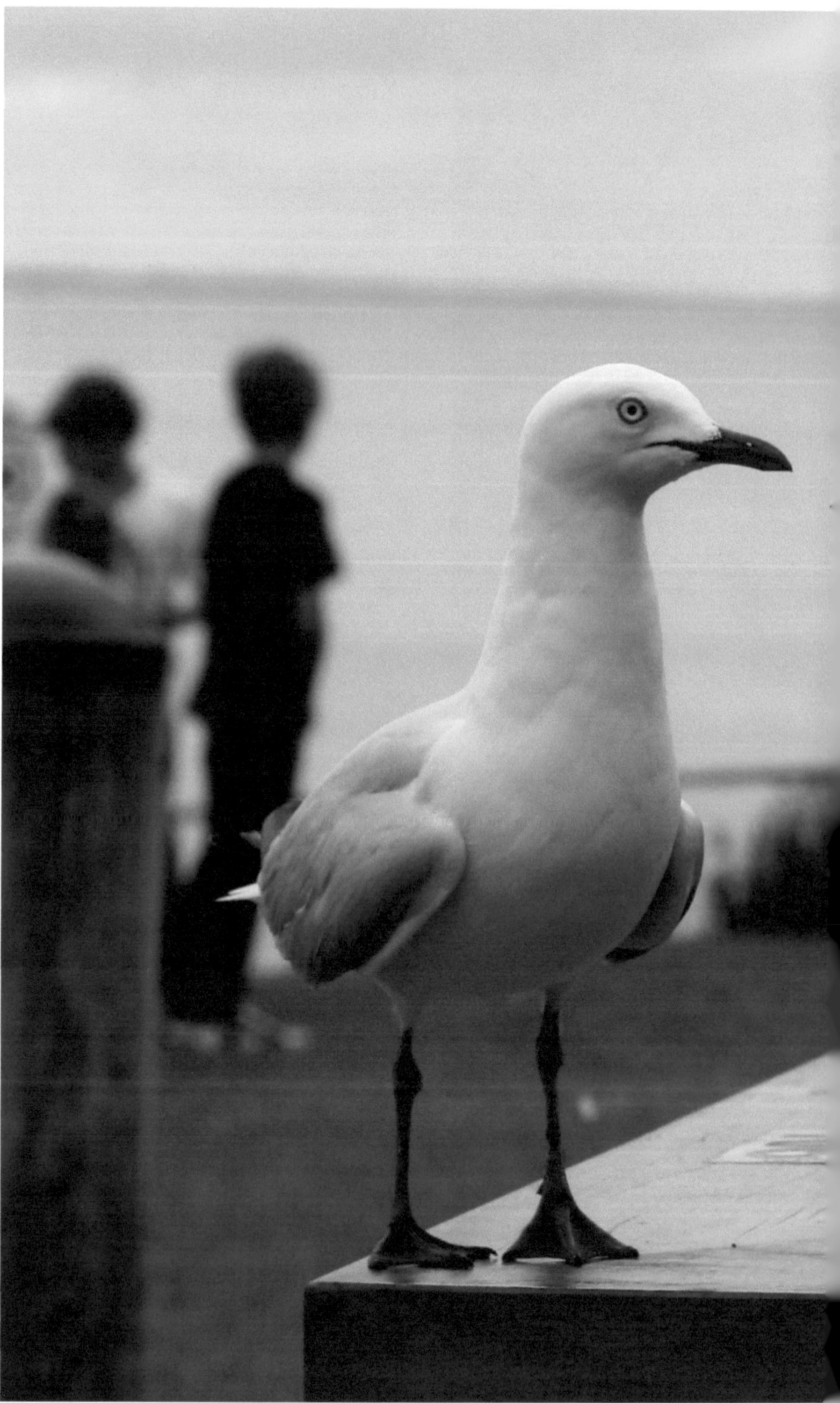

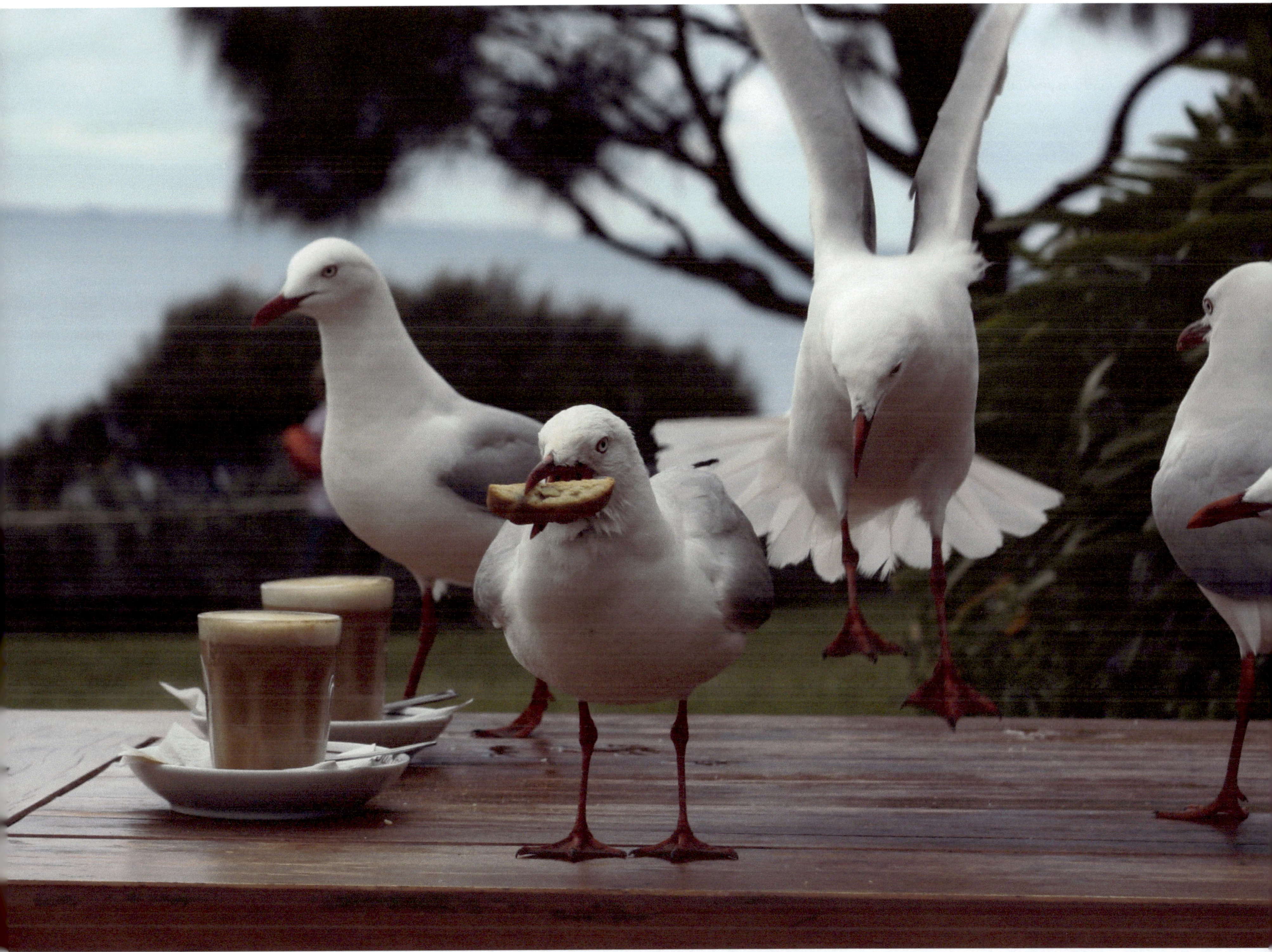

Biographies

Arulanantham Jeevatharshan

I am an avid student of history and culture and love to learn and memorise the stories of the past. I love to take photos of landscapes and natural beauty but my favourite subject is my 3 year old daughter. My greatest job is to document her life. I also want to preserve our history and our heritage for her, so I spend much of my time blogging and participating in activism through social media.

Atiya Karimshah

Atiya is a freelance photographer and artist. You can usually find her somewhere in the outdoors, camera in hand waiting patiently for that perfect shot.

Find her on instagram @atiyaphoto or Facebook: @atiyaiam

Donbosco Prashanth

I love to take photos in my spare time, in fact photography is my favorite hobby. The aim of indulging such an interest is sheer pleasure or relaxation. It is an escape from the day to day grind of work and home. I believe that anyone can be a photographer if they put their mind to it and I have spent time teaching young people to explore their creativity through this medium. I tell my students not to worry if they can not afford the latest equipment, building their skill and imagination should always be the focus of their photography.

Find him on Facebook @BosprashanthPhotography.

Johnny Nguyen

I am a Sydney born artist and photographer of Vietnamese heritage. When I was really young I remember watching my dad paint and draw pictures, as I watched him spend hours and hours on each piece of work, it inspired me to draw. This is probably the point of beginning for me when I knew I wanted to do creative work like him. I love all forms of creative media from visual, audio, physical or digital. One of my favourite creative mediums is photography. The idea of capturing that moment of beauty through your camera and keeping it forever is incredible. Photographs are a visual reference of memories of moments in your life, which can bring many emotions back to you. I want to travel to every corner of the world and take pictures to remember the greatest moments of my journey through life.

Krushanth Thanabalasingam

I am a Sri Lankan born freelance photographer inspired into photography from my early career of artistry. My intention in taking photos is to frame life's little lessons and find a deeper meaning in the everyday. As a photographer I aim to capture unusual angles, so as to provide a perspective that is different to what the naked eye can see. I want my photos to be overlayed with stories that highlight the culture, practice and heritage of the subject.

Mayra Alejandra Abadia Quimbaya

My name is Mayra Alejandra Abadia Quimbaya and I am 20 years. I was born on August 14, 1997 in Cali, Colombia. I live with my mother Cielo and my cats Guero and Violeta. I study social communication and journalism and I love photography. I also like to learn languages and go to the Cinema. In the future I hope to travel around the world and work with photography.
I like to take photos of animals and landscapes so on this occasion I take the photograph of a cute donkey that I saw in the Cocora valley and which has an interesting history behind.

Shabnaaz Ahmed

My name is Shabnaaz and I am a graphic designer and photographer. I am a digital designer by trade but my passion for design keeps my eyes open to all things creative.

Find her on instagram @shab.naaz or Facebook: @isstyle

Trine Vik

I love capturing moments that might otherwise be forgotten and that's one of the reasons I love photography so much. Sometimes I see the world in pictures, like I am always searching for the perfect shot. I like to preserve what is beautiful in this world, because nothing in eternal and beautiful things should be remembered.

Find her on Instagram: @trinedenfine or Facebook: @photosbyvik

www.ingramcontent.com/pod-product-compliance
Lightning Source LLC
Chambersburg PA
CBHW042024050726

47602CB00010B/154